T0356439

SETTLING THE
MISSISSIPPI
TERRITORY

THE ORIGIN OF
TWO STATES

MIKE BUNN AND CLAY WILLIAMS

THE
History
PRESS

The authors dedicate this book to two professors who guided our studies and helped us in our careers. Mike Bunn wishes to recognize the late Dr. Forrest McDonald, a historian and author at the University of Alabama who helped Mike understand the fundamentals of good writing and the duty historians have to share their discoveries with others. Clay Williams would like to thank Dr. John F. Marszalek from Mississippi State University, who greatly influenced his path and helped get him to where he is today.

We also want to jointly thank Elbert Hilliard, the recently deceased director emeritus of the Mississippi Department of Archives and History. Mr. Hilliard will forever stand as a giant in the field of public history and preservation. He served as a mentor early in the authors' careers and provided excellent insight in the production of the Heritage of Mississippi series volume Old Southwest to Old South: Mississippi, 1798–1840 *on which this book is based. He is greatly missed.*

Published by The History Press
Charleston, SC
www.historypress.com

The Mississippi Territory, by Fielding Lucas Jr., 1816. *Courtesy of the David Rumsey Map Collection.*

First published 2025

Manufactured in the United States

ISBN 9781467158794

Library of Congress Control Number: 2024949864

CONTENTS

TIMELINE

OCTOBER 27, 1795
Treaty of San Lorenzo (Pinckney's Treaty) signed.

FEBRUARY 24, 1797
Andrew Ellicott arrives in Natchez.

JULY 1797
"Permanent Committee" formed; first time the area came under American authority.

MARCH 30, 1798
Spanish troops abandon Natchez.

APRIL 7, 1798
Congress creates Mississippi Territory.

AUGUST 1798
Winthrop Sargent arrives as Mississippi's first territorial governor.

FEBRUARY 1799
First territorial laws, "Sargent's Codes," adopted.

MAY 1801
W.C.C. Claiborne appointed second governor of Mississippi.

December 1801
Treaty of Fort Adams, first major treaty between the United States and Choctaw Nation, cedes Choctaw land in the southwestern portion of the Territory and authorizes improvements to the Natchez Trace.

May 1802
Territorial capital moved from Natchez to Washington, Mississippi.

May 1802
Jefferson College chartered.

April 30, 1803
Louisiana Purchase signed.

November 1803
Eastern portion of territory petitions for separation.

December 1803
Claiborne and James Wilkinson journey to New Orleans to accept Louisiana Purchase.

November 1805
Treaty of Washington, signed with the Creeks, allows the construction of what became the Federal Road. Construction begins 1806.

May 13, 1806
Robert Williams becomes governor.

January–February 1807
Aaron Burr Affair.

March 3, 1809
Robert Williams's tenure as governor ends.

June 30, 1809
David Holmes arrives in Natchez to assume governorship.

SEPTEMBER 1810
West Florida Revolt; the next month, the United States annexes the land south of the thirty-first parallel stretching between the Mississippi and Perdido Rivers, even though Spain continues to occupy the region.

JUNE 1812
United States declares war on Great Britain.

JANUARY–APRIL 1813
Andrew Jackson's Natchez Expedition.

APRIL 1813
U.S. troops seize Mobile from the Spanish.

AUGUST 30, 1813
Battle of Fort Mims.

MARCH 27, 1814
Battle of Horseshoe Bend.

AUGUST 9, 1814
Signing of Treaty of Fort Jackson.

DECEMBER 24, 1814
Treaty of Ghent, ending War of 1812, signed.

JANUARY 8, 1815
Battle of New Orleans.

OCTOBER 1816
Pearl River Convention.

MARCH 1, 1817
Enabling Act signed, allowing for the admission of the western portion of territory as the state of Mississippi and reorganizing the eastern section as Alabama Territory.

JULY–AUGUST 1817
Mississippi Constitutional Convention.

DECEMBER 10, 1817
Mississippi becomes the twentieth state in the Union.

JANUARY 19, 1818
Opening of the first meeting of the new Alabama Territory legislature.

MARCH 2, 1819
President James Monroe signs the act, enabling the formation of a state government for Alabama as a first step toward admission into the Union.

JULY–AUGUST 1819
Alabama Constitutional Convention.

DECEMBER 14, 1819
Alabama becomes the twenty-second state to join the Union.

PREFACE

The Mississippi Territory existed as a political entity for nearly two decades. Stretching from the Tennessee border south to the Gulf of Mexico and bounded on the east by the state of Georgia and the west by the mighty Mississippi River, this enormous swath of America's southwestern frontier, in 1817, was divided into the state of Mississippi and the Alabama Territory. Two years later, in 1819, Alabama entered the Union as a state. During an eventful twenty-one-year period, the territory thus transitioned from a sparsely inhabited backwoods frontier to a thriving and dynamic centerpiece in one of the fastest-developing regions of the country.

This territorial period in both states' past, therefore, represents one of the most remarkable and fascinating eras in their long and storied histories. It deserves to be appreciated and understood as a distinct period of their development and maturation. The pattern of development that period witnessed did nothing less than set in motion all that would come after, influencing for generations such basic aspects of the states' development as patterns of land use, the location of their communities and the functioning of their economies and set the tone for the society that grew within their borders. Despite the centrality of the era's importance to Mississippi and Alabama's shared heritage, the territorial era is barely remembered today. The timeline of the events that mark its history are relatively little understood, and when they are mentioned in the region's historiography, they are commonly lumped into the later antebellum period to which it gave birth but had limited connection. There is much to be admired in this story of coming of age, but there is also much to be regretted. The pioneering spirit that animated the early American settlers to lay Mississippi and Alabama's foundation, after all, at the same time facilitated the rise of a society built, in no small part, at the expense of the area's Native inhabitants and the forced labor of enslaved Black people. It is a complicated legacy, to be sure, but it is one that is at the very heart of understanding both states' past.

The authors have spent a large portion of their professional careers researching and writing about this critical formative period. In addition to their work at various cultural heritage institutions in the region, they have written books, articles and other pieces focusing on it and have been given opportunities to speak to groups across both states and beyond about its importance. This book is both a culmination of those years of study and a response to what the authors see as a need for a general overview history of Mississippi and Alabama's territorial period. Nothing like it has ever been published. It is intended to be an introduction to the people, places and events that figured prominently in Mississippi and Alabama's territorial years.

In a fast-paced narrative divided into six short chapters, this book chronicles both states' formative periods. It provides overviews of the Mississippi Territory's contested formation from the remnants of a Spanish colony and the gradual expansion of its boundaries; the tumultuous effort to bring law and order to the region and the colorful characters who guided its political development; the watershed conflict known as the Creek War that raged across it in 1813–14 and the associated international intrigue of the era in which it took place; the fabled "Great Migration" to the Mississippi Territory in the war's aftermath, which began its transformation from frontier to centerpiece in regional development; daily life, society and culture in the territory; and the story behind its division into two dynamic and fast-growing states. It is the authors' goal that this book serves as a reference source on Mississippi's and Alabama's beginnings and inspires readers to learn more about this forgotten chapter in the region's past. To that end, in addition to the chapters of narrative history, the authors have included short biographies of dozens of key individuals from the period, descriptions and locations of key historic sites across Mississippi and Alabama associated with the territorial period and a special section featuring all known maps of the territory produced prior to statehood.

The history of the Mississippi Territory and the short-lived Alabama Territory is a fascinating saga filled with consequential events and colorful characters. The authors hope this book will help readers rediscover this formative era. It is intended to be a starting point for one's understanding and provides readers resources to gain further insight. Narrative history, reference source and travel guide, it is the authors' effort to share their enthusiasm for one of the most intriguing and important interludes in the region's past with the broadest possible audience.

1

RAISING THE AMERICAN FLAG

Nothing signifies the transfer of power like the raising of one's national colors. Andrew Ellicott did just that when he arrived on the scene in Natchez in the late 1790s. He had been sent by the United States government to participate in the survey of the all-important thirty-first parallel, which then served as the border between Spanish Florida and the United States. In the recent Treaty of San Lorenzo (signed 1795), Spain had finally yielded the disputed Yazoo Strip, which consisted of land between the thirty-first parallel and the mouth of the Yazoo River and stretched between the Mississippi and the Chattahoochee Rivers. This finally placed Natchez and its environs within United States territory. When he arrived in Natchez after a long six-month journey, however, the Spanish governor gave no clear indication on when the survey would commence or that his government planned on ceding the territory at all.

Ellicott was anxious to begin marking the boundary and, perhaps even more importantly, assert American control. At his encampment in town, Ellicott, defiantly and emphatically, made the strongest declaration of American authority possible. On February 29, 1797, on a prominent hill in town, Ellicott's men hoisted the United States flag for all to see, boldly proclaiming American authority over the region. Spanish officials were aghast at this affront to their sovereignty and made pleas for the flag to be removed, but Ellicott would not be denied. Tension and discord would reign for the next year as Spanish and American leaders, along with a bevy

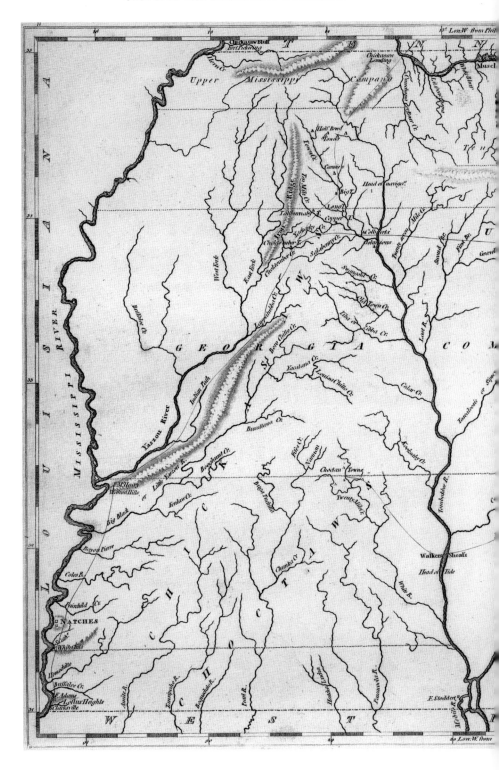

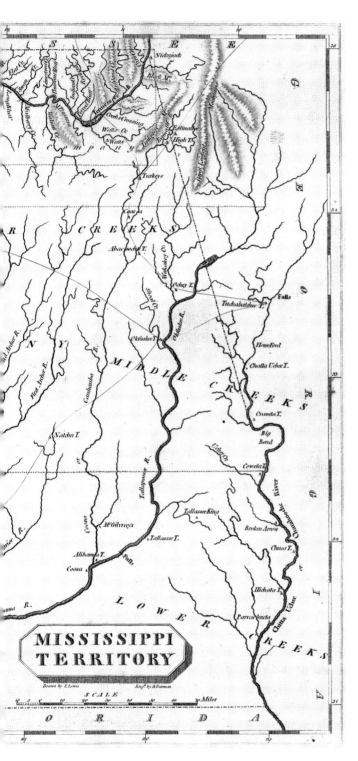

Map of the Mississippi Territory in 1804, showing the thirty-first parallel and the northern border, as observed by the British during their administration of the colony of West Florida. *Courtesy of the David Rumsey Map Collection.*

of characters from the district, struggled for control of the disputed region. It would be a sign of things to come in not only the immediate future but also the tumultuous decades ahead.

Mississippi's beginnings, like most of its history, started with controversy. After the United States won its independence from Great Britain, the 1783 Treaty of Paris established boundaries for the fledgling country. The new nation stretched from the Atlantic Ocean to the Mississippi River and from British Canada in the north all the way to Spanish Florida in the south. Officials from Spain and the United States had different opinions on the location of the northern boundary of Spanish Florida, leading to more than a decade of dispute.

The problem originated with the end of the French and Indian War, at which time the British established the colony of West Florida. The 1763 treaty that ended that war initially set the northern boundary of this British possession at the thirty-first parallel. A year later, Great Britain moved the boundary northward to 32° 28', the point where the Yazoo River runs into the Mississippi River. During the Revolutionary War, Spain fought against Great Britain in an effort to win back some of its former possessions and took control of West Florida through military conquest. In the 1783 Treaty of Paris, Britain officially ceded its Florida possessions to Spain but without any clear mention of the northern boundary. The United States felt the boundary should be placed at the thirty-first parallel, the original northern boundary of West Florida. The Spanish, on the other hand, felt the line lay farther north at the limit the British themselves had claimed upon their capture of the province.

The major difference between these two boundaries as it concerned the development of the region lay in who could claim ownership of the Natchez District, the rich agricultural region along the Mississippi River's lower reaches containing some of the few thriving European settlements in what historians now refer to as the Old Southwest. This frontier region, literally south and west of the nation's more populous Eastern Seaboard, is roughly defined as all the territory stretching between the Ocmulgee River in Georgia and south of the Tennessee River. Containing approximately two thousand residents, the Natchez District had become an important area to Spanish officials and had become coveted by the United States.

The State of Georgia added to the confusion that existed in 1783 by claiming the Mississippi River as its own western boundary. Two years later, by legislative enactment, Georgia officially created Bourbon County in the

Natchez District. Spain therefore had to fend off encroachment from the national government of the United States and the rogue state of Georgia.

Spain would spend the next decade attempting to consolidate its control over the area through a number of methods, such as establishing strong relations with the region's Natives, constructing several strategically located forts and, most importantly, developing the town of Natchez into a more permanent settlement to serve as a population and government center. Spanish leaders established a liberal land grant policy and did not force Catholicism, the official religion of Spain and its colonies, on the local citizens. Although confronted by an ever-expanding United States eager to take control over the region that they thought should be theirs legally, Spanish leaders, in the mid-1790s, were pleased with their efforts at strengthening their hold. They would soon be stunned to learn their efforts had been wasted.

Spain's control of the Natchez District officially ended with the Treaty of San Lorenzo, signed on October 27, 1795. Also known as Pinckney's Treaty (named after negotiator Thomas Pinckney), this accord settled the longstanding controversy over the boundary issue when Spain accepted the thirty-first parallel as the boundary between Spanish Florida and the United States. Just as importantly, the treaty also allowed Americans free navigation of the Mississippi River and the right of deposit in New Orleans. Traders would no longer have to pay duties to store merchandise in New Orleans before shipping items elsewhere.

First page of the Treaty of San Lorenzo. *Courtesy of the Library of Congress.*

Local Spanish colonial officials were totally uncommitted to following the terms of the treaty, however, and the population was confused and worried about the future. The region's inhabitants also had mixed feelings regarding their new rulers. Many settlers preferred Spanish rule, as they had prospered under their policies, and they were apprehensive about change. Others, however, looked forward to American control and the benefits they thought it would bring. These circumstances called for level-headed leadership to manage these affairs during this period of transition. The situation got Andrew Ellicott instead.

Born in 1754 in Pennsylvania to a Quaker family, Andrew Ellicott had acquired vast experience in the surveying profession, including work on the famous Mason-Dixon line and the establishment of boundaries between Georgia and North Carolina and Ohio and Pennsylvania. For all his skills and experience, he did, however, lack the necessary tact to handle the important job given to him. President George Washington commissioned him to be the nation's representative to survey and mark the boundary between Spanish possessions and the United States. He garnered instructions and advice from Secretary of State Timothy Pickering, who told him of the importance of maintaining peace with the Spanish and the neighboring Natives. In meetings with President Washington, Ellicott had been warned to prevent Spain from delaying the implementation of the treaty and advised to be wary of Americans working with the Spanish government, which was trying to detach western states from the American Union. Ellicott did not possess the experience that would have equipped him to handle this delicate diplomatic situation. Confusion existed about who exactly was to take charge of the territory and establish control for the United States. Was this Ellicott's function or perhaps that of military commanders sent to take possession of Spanish forts in the region? It would become apparent that Ellicott was more than willing to take the responsibility on himself.

ANDREW ELLICOTT.
Born 1754.—Died 1820.

Andrew Ellicott. *Courtesy of the Library of Congress.*

Tensions between Ellicott and local Spanish Governor Manuel Gayoso de Lemos began from the start. Ellicott had heard on his journey south that the Spanish never intended to honor the terms of the treaty, and his attempt to force the Spanish to acknowledge American ownership by hoisting the flag of the United States only added to the stress. Gayoso claimed he wanted the flag removed for fear that the Natives would become unruly, but considering the disregard for the treaty's enforcement he had already seen on his journey south, Ellicott must not have believed him. Ellicott began pestering Gayoso immediately to "name a day on which our operations should commence," meaning: When could the boundary be properly marked so the Spanish could withdraw from United States territory?[1]

Gayoso gave various reasons for delaying the enforcement of the treaty, but Ellicott was not to be denied and proved persistent in his desire for action, sometimes sending three notes a day to Gayoso. As time went by, Ellicott sensed Gayoso and the Spanish were not moving toward evacuation. At one point, he even witnessed cannon being removed from the fort at Natchez, only to be returned days later. Gayoso felt that Ellicott was agitating settlers, while Ellicott claimed tensions were rising simply because of Spanish insincerity in executing the treaty and evacuating. The situation was turning critical, and like other tense historical events, all it needed was a spark to ignite a flame.

That spark came in June from an unlikely source: an itinerant Baptist preacher named Barton Hannon. After conducting a sermon, Hannon entered a religious controversy in a part of town generally inhabited, at that time, by Irish Roman Catholics who took offense at the manner in which Hannon condemned the tenets of their church. They proceeded to give him a beating. After the altercation, Hannon met with Gayoso and demanded justice. Gayoso eventually felt threatened by the preacher and proceeded to throw him in jail. On his way to incarceration, Hannon yelled, "Help me, fellow Americans!" as he passed by Ellicott's camp. The seed for rebellion had been sowed.[2]

Events then began to fall into place rapidly. A few days after Hannon's jailing, on June 12, over three hundred men gathered at Belk's Tavern on the Natchez Trace to discuss freeing Hannon and organizing a revolt. Some advocated immediate assault, but Ellicott discouraged it. A few brave souls decided to approach the fort to consult with Spanish leaders, despite rumors it had been rigged with mines, only to be turned away and be fired upon. The danger so alarmed Gayoso that he moved himself and his family inside the fort for safety. A short time later, a committee of citizens sent a letter to Gayoso with a list of demands in order to restore peace. This began the process of virtually ending Spanish control over the Natchez District with the establishment of a governing body known as a "Permanent Committee."

It proved to be a major mistake to create a governing body without clearly defined responsibilities and duties. Leading the uproar was Anthony Hutchins. Described as a man of "unlimited ambition" and "of an active, restless, and discontented spirit," Hutchins declared war on this new governing committee. Hutchins complained the committee had not been duly mandated and authorized and would be only the tool of Ellicott, whom Hutchins despised. So, in quick fashion, Hutchins tried to dissolve the committee himself. Gaining permission from acting Governor Stephen

Minor, Hutchins secured authorization for new elections in September, which led to the formation of a Committee of Safety and Correspondence. Gayoso had left his post in late July to assume another post in New Orleans. With Spanish control all but ended, two distinct factions vied to discredit the other and take a leadership role in rule of the district. Ellicott and Hutchins would lead the respective groups in these endeavors. Ellicott's group (the Permanent Committee) was composed mainly of newcomers, merchants and former favorites of the Spanish regime, whereas Hutchins's faction (the Committee of Safety) composed mostly long-term residents, indebted famers and opponents of Ellicott. After both factions formed, Ellicott and Hutchins went round and round with episodes that would be comedic if not for the realization of the damage they did to the tranquility in the district.

The arrival of Captain Isaac Guion in late 1797 began calming matters. Guion had been assigned to take possession of certain posts held by Spanish garrisons. Upon Guion's arrival, it did not take him long to assess the situation and determine that neither committee was good for the region. In a letter to the secretary of state in February 1798, Guion stated, "The inhabitants of this Country are very anxious for the establishment of some government from the executive of the United States." Guion obviously thought the situation would not dramatically improve until a legitimate government could be established. That could not happen until the Spanish completely evacuated.[3]

Spanish leadership finally determined that their hopes of holding on to this district had ended, and the time had come to evacuate. On March 23, the Spanish evacuated Fort Nogales at present-day Vicksburg, and on March 30, Ellicott recorded in his journal, "I rose...at five o'clock and walked to the fort, and found the last party, or rear guard just leaving it....I went in, and enjoyed from the parapet, the pleasing prospects of gallies and boats leaving the shore and getting underway. They were out of sight of the town before daylight." Guion sent official word that same day: "I have the honor to announce to your Excellency the evacuation of the posts of Walnut Hills and Natchez by the troops of his Catholic Majesty....I have put a small guard in this post & the flag of the U. States now is waving over the rampart." Over one hundred years of rule by various European nations in Natchez had finally ended.[4]

With the Spanish evacuation concluded and Guion now maintaining order himself, Ellicott was finally able to proceed with his original mission to survey and mark the thirty-first parallel. Working with representatives of the Spanish government, Ellicott began the process of marking the 381

Top: Mississippi River at Natchez. *Courtesy of the Library of Congress.*

Bottom: *View of Natchez*, circa 1822, by John James Audubon. *Historic Natchez Foundation.*

The Ellicott Stone. *Photograph by Mike Bunn.*

miles between the Mississippi and Chattahoochee Rivers. The job proved as difficult as it sounded, as the surveyors faced not only hostile Natives but also "mosquitoes, malaria, canebrakes, torrential rains, and incompetent helpers." Once the survey was completed, Ellicott finally returned north to Philadelphia, where he had his journal published in 1803; it provided a fascinating account of this transitionary period.[5]

During these calamitous times, the U.S. government made arrangements to establish authority in the region, and Congress created the Mississippi Territory on April 7, 1798. The act established boundaries for the territory, which consisted of lands north of the thirty-first parallel and south of the mouth of Yazoo River and east of Mississippi River and west of the Chattahoochee River. The act also established a government like the one created for the Northwest Territory, but unlike that act, it did not forbid the institution of slavery, which already existed and whose illegality would have been challenged by the region's residents.

The territory's government structure would play a huge role in the events to come. The president, with the consent of Congress, would appoint a governor, secretary and three judges, who could adopt laws and appoint civil and militia officers. Once the territory's population included five thousand free adult men, an assembly could be elected, and a delegate could be sent to Congress. This created a very nondemocratic form of government to control a district that had already had its share of authority issues. Anyone with foresight could have predicted the results to come.

The choice of the territory's first governor would only add fuel to the fire. President John Adams selected Winthrop Sargent for the post. Sargent had many suitable qualifications for the job. He had a strong military background, with service during the Revolutionary War and against the Natives in the Northwest, and territorial administrative experience, as he had served for ten years as secretary of the Northwest Territory. George Washington himself even wrote a testimonial, stating he "displayed a zeal, integrity and intelligence which did honor him as an officer and a gentleman." Sargent had some attributes, however, that would not mesh with the residents of his new frontier environment. Sargent was a strict Puritan from Massachusetts who abhorred frontier standards of morality and the institution of slavery. His Federalist views of the need for a strong centralized government also conflicted with a democratic-loving society unaccustomed to a vigorous governmental presence.[6]

Aside from these personality differences, Sargent faced a monumental task. The biggest issue Sargent had to solve involved land issues. France, England and Spain had all issued land grants in the region, and the new government had to sort out these overlapping and sometimes conflicting claims. Georgia also complicated matters, as that state had claimed much of that land going back to the 1780s. In 1789 and 1795, the Georgia legislature passed the Yazoo Land Acts, which granted millions of acres of land in the region to private land companies that then sold land to settlers and speculators.

Secondly, most of the territory was inhabited by various Native nations who were apprehensive after their ally Spain abandoned them to the ever-expanding United States. Sargent's new government would have to maintain peace between these tribes and land-hungry immigrants. The Spanish had cemented their friendship with the Natives through the giving of gifts, and the new government lacked the money to continue this process. Sargent had nothing to offer and complained that many residents "were literally eaten out of house and home."[7]

Adopting laws became another important issue. Sargent needed the help of his judges, and as historian Robert Haynes has said, "Territorial judges were slow to arrive, loath to remain on the job, and eager to leave." One judge resided in the area, but the second did not arrive until January 1799, and only then did Sargent feel he could begin adopting laws. The writing of these laws would cause tremendous divisiveness in the community.[8]

Finally, the need to maintain order stood as crucial. The area had long been a refuge for escaped prisoners, border ruffians, fugitive murderers and heavily burdened debtors, and Sargent needed to appoint sheriffs and justices of the peace to deal with issues of disorder. As an indicator of the importance of this regulation, one of the first public buildings constructed in the territory by the new American government was a jail in Natchez. On top of this, setting up a militia for the territory's defense was of utmost concern. A strong militia was important to providing safety from possible Native attacks, as well as meeting any potential threat from European nations.

After a tumultuous period of transition, the United States had finally removed the Spanish from their newly acquired territory and established an official government. Residents were anxious to put the problems of the past aside and move toward solving the issues at hand. It would soon be clear the new American rule would not put an end to this divisive environment. In fact, it would only get worse before it got better.

2

RIVALRIES, FACTIONS AND FIGHTS

Throughout the nearly twenty years of its existence, the Mississippi Territory was racked by bitter political factionalism. This turmoil existed prior to the United States assuming control, but it became amplified with the arrival of Governor Winthrop Sargent. In his initial address, Sargent laid out his priorities when he stressed the need for "a concise and clear code of laws, intelligible to the most common capacity," which would be executed with uniformity and fairness. He also told the crowd that the right to own property in enslaved people would be continued, appointments would be made and a militia would be established. He meant for the speech to serve as an introduction to the principles by which he planned to govern the new territory, but his talk of creating "good citizens void of Jealousy of each other and emulous of public good" would soon prove ironic.[9]

Jealousies would soon arise, as Sargent decided to visit with several local citizens to gain an understanding of the community and the political environment. One of the first people he met with was Andrew Ellicott. Sargent wanted his opinion on the leading men of the district so he could make proper appointments. Sargent could not have made a poorer decision regarding whom he placed his trust in, as there was no more divisive a personality than Ellicott.

Sargent moved quickly to establish his government. With other officials slow to arrive, he was forced to operate by executive decree. He appointed minor officials, such as sheriffs, and created necessary offices, such as a

Winthrop Sargent. *Courtesy of the Mississippi Department of Archives and History.*

probate court to administer estates. In so doing, he chose two of Ellicott's favorites as judges. Sargent also organized the militia and appointed officers. His choices of individuals to fill these positions caused some rumblings, but matters got even more contentious when Sargent moved to create a set of laws. By January 1799, two judges had assumed their positions, so Sargent felt it was time to establish a legal code for the territory. Sargent proved hesitant, however, as he felt himself and the other two judges lacked adequate knowledge to formulate the laws. The critical issue became whether Sargent and his officials were simply adopting laws or creating new ones. So, without any strong set of laws to use as a model, they "made" laws instead of adopting ones. This decision would generate problems in the future.

By the end of February 1799, forty-six new laws, which soon became known derisively as "Sargent's Codes," had been drafted. These laws established rules and regulations for militia and various court systems; defined crimes and their punishments; and regulated marriages and taverns. These laws made many of Sargent's executive decrees official and were in accordance with his strong desire to install order in a district that had, for too long, been lacking in such regard. These new laws would send his rapidly growing list of opponents into a frenzy.

Opposition to Sargent grew quickly. Long-time agitator Anthony Hutchins had finally grown too old and infirm to cause too much ruckus, so he passed the mantle on to others in his camp, principally Thomas Marston Green and Cato West, who had married into the Green family. These opponents would become known as the "Green-West Faction" or the "West Junto." Sargent, unfortunately, did not do much to foster support for himself as tensions rose. His strict Puritan ways and haughty attitude did not sit well with many of the region's inhabitants, and his desire to establish strict law and order was not embraced either. No "man so frigid and sour" could ever gain friends and allies with "free people."[10]

Opponents of Sargent drafted a petition to Congress to lay out their concerns. The appeal listed several problems with the current government in the Mississippi Territory. Besides discussing the right of citizens to have their own voice in government, the main focus of the petition centered on the arbitrary mingling of "executive, legislative, and Judicial authorities" in the hands of "three or four individuals." The solution proposed was simple: grant the territory the second stage of government, which would provide a bicameral legislature. The petition found allies in Congress, including William C.C. Claiborne of Tennessee, who sponsored legislation that moved the territory into the second stage of government.[11]

Sargent had no choice but to conduct elections for the general assembly, although he was convinced that the region's inhabitants were "unfitted in every view of the matter for that second stage of Order." And to further cement his disappointment and anger, the electorate voted in eight of his harshest critics, including West, Green and Anthony Hutchins himself. Sargent did not have to deal with an oppositional legislature for long because his fate soon became sealed. Thomas Jefferson's election as president in

THOMAS JEFFERSON,

Vice President of the U.S.

Left: Thomas Jefferson. *Courtesy of the Library of Congress.*

Right: W.C.C. Claiborne. *Courtesy of the Library of Congress.*

1800 signaled an end to his term. The Republican Jefferson felt the need to satisfy many of his supporters' wishes and appointed W.C.C. Claiborne to replace Sargent.[12]

Whereas Sargent's background provided ample experience for assuming this position, the young Claiborne's résumé was not quite as impressive. A native of Virginia, the twenty-six-year-old served as a congressional clerk, as a member of Tennessee's first constitutional convention and on the Tennessee Supreme Court. Appointed in May 1801, he arrived in Natchez that November. If he had hopes that, with Sargent's departure, the political climate would settle down, he was soon disappointed.

Upon his arrival, Claiborne gave an address to the legislative body in December that summarized his priorities and goals for the future. He expressed the need for improvements with the judicial department and a strong concern for the formation of a proper militia amid constant fears of Native attack, slave revolts and meddling by the Spanish. These issues and the continual struggle to resolve land disputes would dominate much of his time in office. He "formed a firm Resolution to exercise the authority vested in me" and discussed how "Party Spirit, that Bane to happiness," was not in the best interest of man and the community.[13]

Disregarding Claiborne's call for harmony, the legislature quickly fanned the flames of discord. They moved the capital away from Federalist-dominated Natchez six miles up the road to the new town of Washington. They changed the county name of Pickering (named after Secretary of State Timothy Pickering, another hated Federalist) to Jefferson, and they repealed most of the hated "Sargent's Codes."

Plenty of other examples of factionalism occurred during Claiborne's tenure. Rival literary and cultural societies were formed; Republicans led by the Green family established the Mississippi Republican Society, while Federalists created the Mississippi Society for the Acquisition and Dissemination of Useful Knowledge. Partisan newspapers were also launched in this era. Federalists started the territory's first newspaper, the *Mississippi Herald*, while Claiborne sought out others to print laws, circulars and handbills.

Bickering also delayed the establishment of an important educational institution. Claiborne called for a "seminary of learning," and the legislature responded by incorporating Jefferson College in May 1802. The legislation, however, provided no source of funding and left it up to donations to get the school off the ground. This, in turn, led to disagreement over where to place the school. It was not until 1811 that classes finally began at Jefferson College, which had been located in Washington. This entire controversy simply revealed that there were two Republican factions (Claiborne's group and the Green/West Junto) and shoved Claiborne closer to the old-line Federalists.

Claiborne had his hands full regardless of the constant political squabbles. He received help on the ever-present land issue when the U.S. government, in 1802, finally convinced Georgia to give up its claims on western lands. The following year, Congress passed a monumental land act that validated land claims prior to the Treaty of San Lorenzo (Pinckney's Treaty) and established a system for selling of other lands. Issues with the Spanish to the south would also dominate Claiborne's term. Spanish officials closed the port of New Orleans in 1802, causing great concerns. Word that Spain had secretly sold Louisiana to the French made matters worse. Spanish possession of southern lands was one thing, but Napoleon controlling the area economically as well as politically was something else entirely. Fortunately, French reverses

Jefferson College. *Photograph by Clay Williams.*

in Europe and on the island of Saint Dominique led the French emperor to sell all of France's Louisiana possessions to the United States. President Jefferson sent Claiborne to officially accept the colony in December 1803. He did not know it at the time, but Claiborne would not return to his post, as he eventually became Louisiana's governor. He would find new challenges there but was probably happy to put Mississippi behind him.

The constant factionalism in the Mississippi Territory was not only related to people and party but was sectional as well. Washington County is a case in point. Established in 1800, the county encompassed an enormous area of territory east of the Pearl River. Separated by three hundred miles from the government in Natchez, its residents felt isolated and neglected. Court proceedings seldom occurred, and the economy struggled. Residents exporting their products down the rivers to Mobile had to pay high duties to the Spanish. Failing to get their grievances heard, residents petitioned Congress for separation from the Mississippi Territory in November 1803. It was the first mention of the possibility of splitting the territory, but it was far from the last and became an issue every future governor was forced to deal with in one way or another.

Upon Claiborne's departure, Territorial Secretary Cato West assumed executive duties. Ambitious to a fault and leader of the Green-West faction, West now assumed his dream position and, with powerful friends and family, assumed he would be appointed to the position on a permanent basis. To his utter despair, West did not get his wish. Thomas Jefferson eventually appointed Robert Williams as governor. In perhaps the greatest example of sour political grapes from the era, West promptly returned to his estate in Greenville and took the official government records with him. It took threats from the territorial assembly to finally force him to relinquish the papers.

Williams, Mississippi's third territorial governor, was a North Carolina native and a former congressman. He was serving as land commissioner for the district west of the Pearl River at the time of his appointment. Upon accepting the job from President Thomas Jefferson, he requested to continue to hold onto that lucrative position and also asked permission to return to his native state for personal business. Both of these decisions caused friction with his new fellow residents. And Williams needed no further strikes against him, as his temperament did him no favors.

Williams made the same wrong assumption that his predecessor made concerning political stability once Winthrop Sargent left office. Williams explained that "Colonel West has had his political frolic, and all things are quiet." Political tensions would not settle, and upon Williams leaving for North Carolina, one of the territorial period's most intriguing and divisive events took place.[14]

Aaron Burr, along with several boats full of "adventurers," arrived in the territory in January 1807. The former vice president's political career had basically disintegrated after he killed Alexander Hamilton in a duel in 1804. Since then, rumors had run rampant concerning an alleged scheme masterminded by Burr involving the separation of a few states, such as Tennessee and Kentucky, from the rest of the Union and the invasion and capture of Spanish lands where he'd then declare himself ruler. General James Wilkinson, who also offered his services to the Spanish Crown as a paid spy, was rumored to be involved. When Wilkinson heard his name also being mentioned prominently in this plot, he decided to turn on his coconspirator. The climate in the area was filled with uncertainty and unrest.

With Governor Williams gone to tend to his personal affairs, Secretary Cowles Mead served as acting governor. Another ambitious politician, Mead had become a member of the Green faction when he married into the family. Not trusting Wilkinson or Burr, he activated the militia, stirring up more intrigue. He had orders issued for Burr to appear before a grand jury to determine if there was sufficient evidence for his indictment on charges of treason. When he learned of his impending arrest, Burr voluntarily surrendered to territorial authorities in exchange for a guarantee of a trial

in the Mississippi Territory. Burr was released on bond with a court date set for the following month.

Burr's time in the territory served as another example of the factionalism of the times. Several balls were held in his honor, as many residents, including Federalists, were in awe of the famous Burr and were in favor of taking land from the Spanish. Others, however, were anxious to put Burr on trial for treason. Williams eventually returned to assume his duties, and his presence seemed to calm the town. The grand jury indictment hearing took place in Washington, which had never experienced such an event, overloading it with curious visitors. The grand jury absolved Burr and condemned Mead's heavy-handed actions. Judge Rodney was upset and still wanted to see Burr held under his recognizance. Burr, still fearful of getting captured by Wilkinson, fled, only to be later captured and arrested near Mobile. He eventually stood trial in Richmond, where he was acquitted in a landmark verdict that set the precedent for trials involving treason.

Although Burr was out of the picture, things continued to heat up in the Mississippi Territory. Cowles Mead, stinging from the results of the Burr trial, still hoped to claim the governorship for himself. He withdrew from Williams's administration and formed a new faction with notables George Poindexter, a recent arrival in the territory who rose rapidly in local politics, and Ferdinand Claiborne, militia leader and brother to the former governor. Poindexter got elected as a delegate to Congress and quickly worked on petitions to remove Williams from office. In an example of the strong personal animosity involved, Poindexter challenged Williams to a duel because of remarks the governor made about the militia. Williams declined the offer, however, due to his official obligations.

Opposite, left: Aaron Burr. *Courtesy of the Library of Congress.*

Opposite, right: George Poindexter. *Courtesy of the Library of Congress.*

Left: David Holmes. *Courtesy of the Mississippi Department of Archives and History.*

Meanwhile, Mead and Claiborne soon got elected to the legislature and caused problems for Williams on that front.

Williams did not sit quietly while his foes maneuvered around him. Williams took the offensive by removing opposition government officials and militia officers, angering everyone and also causing a rash of resignations in protest. Judge Thomas Rodney wrote to Poindexter, "The Conduct of the Govr Indeed is like That of a Man whose mind is deranged." Williams's strongest attempt to secure his power was his dismissal of the legislature three times in a span of four months. Growing disheartened with the entire affair, Williams finally decided he would leave office when his sponsor Thomas Jefferson moved on. Virginian David Holmes was chosen to replace him. When Williams left Mississippi, he dissolved the assembly yet again. His enemies did not seem to care, as legislators had quite a "frolic," celebrating by parading through the streets of Washington.[15]

David Holmes arrived on June 30, 1809, to begin his term as the Mississippi Territory's fourth governor. It had been a tumultuous decade dominated by constant political discord, but the area finally had a leader who would calm the stormy waters. Pennsylvanian by birth, he had served twelve years in Congress, which perhaps honed his compromising skills. To his benefit, Holmes had a more pleasant and agreeable personality than his predecessors. Robert Haynes compared him adeptly by saying, "He lacked the aloofness of Sargent, the intense ambition and youthful vigor of Claiborne, the egotism of West, the flamboyance of Mead, and the arbitrariness of Williams." Holmes summed it up in a letter he sent to the president soon after his arrival, in which said he hoped to "cherish peace and good will among the people."[16]

Luckily for him, several factors led to a decreased atmosphere of strained factionalism. Several long-term agitators, such as Anthony Hutchins and Thomas M. Green, had passed away. Many had simply faded away from public office or chosen to no longer antagonize the governor. More importantly, people's attention turned to other important events and circumstances. The growing population of the eastern counties threatened the power base of those along the river. Fears of the eastern section of the territory separating to form its own state became more of a possible reality, and citizens wondered how these new population trends would affect the path to statehood. Finally, international affairs also took center stage. Wars in Europe with Napoleon had a harmful effect on the United States, especially its maritime trade and the economy. These important issues finally outweighed petty personal differences and individual pursuits of power.

One could easily summarize government in the Mississippi Territory in three words: bitter political factionalism. Various historians have attempted to state the reasons for such tension, but historian William B. Hamilton said it best when he summarized the political environment of Mississippi's and Alabama's births: "Desire for office and power, petty geographical jealousies and sectionalism, the colonial relation with the United States, and personal and family relationship were the driving forces. They were, so to speak, what the shouting was all about."[17]

3

WARS AND RUMORS OF WARS

The interconnected Creek War and War of 1812 served as the landmark events in Mississippi's territorial period. The results of these conflicts forever altered the political and economic landscape in the territory and did more than all previous efforts to pave the way for statehood. To understand their consequences, it is important to grasp how and why the Creek War occurred, its relationship with the larger War of 1812 and how both impacted the Mississippi Territory.

For decades prior to the outbreak of the Creek War, Americans, Creek Natives and the Spanish had maintained an uneasy truce as they each claimed portions of the Gulf South. Pressure on this shaky arrangement steadily mounted during the early nineteenth century as the region witnessed increased American migration, strained efforts at cultural adaptation on the part of the Creeks and international intrigue associated with the Spanish and their newfound allies, the British. When violence finally erupted, it quickly spiraled into a cataclysmic war that would become a turning point in American history.

The Creek Nation occupied territory located primarily in the eastern section of the Mississippi Territory and Georgia. As a consequence of their location, the Creeks had long been courted by both the Americans and the Spanish for economic and military alliances. While Americans jealously looked on rich Creek lands as perfectly suited for large-scale agriculture, the Spanish simply hoped to use the Creek Nation as a buffer to American encroachment into their territory. As each party pursued its own interests, conflict inevitably resulted.

These concerns only grew over covert British attempts to undermine the safety of the American Gulf South frontier with the outbreak of the War of 1812. Though many of the provocations listed by President James Madison in his call for war, including the longstanding British policy of impressing U.S. sailors and Britain's refusal to evacuate forts on American soil per the terms of the treaty ending the Revolutionary War, were only peripheral concerns of most residents of the Mississippi Territory, the threat of a British-Spanish alliance that would enlist the support of southern Native tribes was one of their greatest fears. The British were believed to have instigated Natives to violence against American settlers in the Northwest, and their increasingly close relationship with the Spanish on the southern frontier caused considerable alarm.

James Madison. *Courtesy of the Library of Congress.*

Caught in the middle of this international intrigue were the Creek Natives, who had been the special focus of a concerted American effort to assimilate Natives since the 1790s. The Creek Nation was a loose confederacy of many smaller tribes representing dozens of towns, politically aligned by geography into "Upper" and "Lower" towns. Many Upper Creeks lived in what is today north-central and northeast Alabama along the Coosa and Tallapoosa River systems, while the Lower Creeks lived primarily along the lower Chattahoochee and Flint River systems. Federal agent Benjamin Hawkins spearheaded the United States government's effort to convince the Creeks to adopt tenets of American society in place of traditional ways that were viewed as incompatible with modern reality. Essential to this plan was the undertaking of staple agriculture in place of hunting; the rationale being that the Creeks would need less land to live on, and vast expanses of their former hunting grounds could therefore be opened to American settlement. The plan, based on cold calculation as much as any altruistic motives, ultimately served to highlight growing divisions in Creek society. The Creeks who embraced the plan were forced to simultaneously and completely reject their ancestral way of life. Furthermore, adoption of the plan by only portions of the Creek population caused previously nonexistent divisions in tribal society, based on ownership of property, to develop. Further straining

Creek-American relations was the construction of the Federal Road. A government-sponsored route through the heart of Creek territory, the road had been designed as an essential link in a road system that would ultimately connect the nation's capital with the vital port city of New Orleans. Many Creeks watched with growing apprehension as thousands of white settlers and their enslaved laborers made their way through their homeland over the route. With growing American interference in their culture, their government and seemingly every aspect of their daily lives, members of the Creek Nation were divided over what course of action to take.

Into this tense situation, in 1811, entered the Shawnee Chief Tecumseh, the proverbial spark that would ultimately ignite the smoldering tinderbox that was the Old Southwest. Claiming familial ties to the Creeks, Tecumseh hailed from the Great Lakes Region and had become a leading figure in Native resistance to American settlement in the Old Northwest. Along with his brother Tenskwatawa (The Prophet), Tecumseh believed a Native confederacy held promise as the only way to ensure the survival of Native tribes in the face of mounting encroachment on their lands by Americans. In the summer and fall of 1811, he traveled throughout the Southeast in an attempt to rally the Chickasaws, Choctaws and Creeks to his cause. He proved largely unsuccessful with the Choctaws and Chickasaws due to the efforts of Choctaw Chief Pushmataha, who counseled his fellow Natives not to be deceived by Tecumseh's message.

Tecumseh found a more receptive audience with the Upper Creeks, many of whom he addressed at the Creek annual council meeting at Tuckaubatchee on the banks of the Tallapoosa River in the eastern section of the Mississippi Territory. While no transcript of his speech survives, evidence strongly suggests he urged abandonment of "American" styles of agriculture and a return to traditional folkways, even if doing so might lead to armed conflict with the United States. Regardless of the exact wording, the message was clear and timely for those inclined to agree with his call.

Heightened tension between Red Sticks, or those who were prepared to take up the symbolic red stick of war, and Creeks friendly to American interests soon erupted into a civil war that fractured Creek society. These clashes between rival Creek factions eventually led to conflict with American frontier settlers who became entangled in this struggle over the future of the Creek people. Violence between Red Sticks and American settlers first flared up in the spring of 1812. During that year, Red Sticks launched several attacks on American settlers living in isolated frontier communities in Mississippi Territory and beyond. With open warfare seemingly inevitable, officials within the Mississippi Territory began to mobilize forces to respond in case of emergency by the summer of 1813.

Nowhere did this state of alarm appear more pronounced than in the southwestern portion of Creek territory north of Mobile. This area, centered near the confluence of the Alabama and Tombigbee Rivers, was a virtual island of American settlement. It contained a large population of mixed-race Creeks who were increasingly viewed with contempt by the Red Sticks. The nearest sizable town, Mobile, lay well to the south. More importantly, it was separated by several hundred miles of wilderness from the seat of the Mississippi territorial government in Washington along the Mississippi River. Keenly aware of their precarious situation, area settlers began to construct a series of stockades for their protection as they prepared for what they believed was an inevitable conflict.

Long-simmering tensions erupted into open conflict between American and Red Stick forces in July 1813. A group of Red Stick warriors, returning from a trip to Pensacola, where they had hoped to obtain arms and ammunition from the Spanish, fought a small force of Mississippi Territorial militia near a small stream known as Burnt Corn Creek. Although the Red Sticks were initially scattered in disorder, they soon rallied and counterattacked while the militia stopped to inspect the plunder they had just captured. The American militia fled in terror. The victory gave the Red Sticks a newfound confidence in their martial abilities. Simultaneously, American forces had been embarrassed and humbled. Aware of the defeat by the militia, many terrified residents fled to the safety of makeshift forts and awaited the probable Red Stick offensive. What happened next at Fort Mims sent shockwaves throughout the nation and seared the volatile situation in the Mississippi Territory into the nation's consciousness.

Fort Mims had been built around several structures on the plantation of planter Samuel Mims. It featured split log walls, two gates and a partially constructed blockhouse in addition to the Mims's plantation outbuildings and several rude cabins constructed by area settlers who had come there for safety. A group of approximately seven hundred Red Sticks advanced on Fort Mims. Though several individuals detected their movement and reported it to the fort commander, Major Daniel Beasley, he refused to believe that Red Sticks were planning an attack on his post. As a consequence of his false sense of confidence, the fort lay totally unprepared for the attack.

On August 30, 1813, hundreds of Red Stick warriors launched a surprise assault on the fort. They went unnoticed until they were within a few steps of the stockade, and they took those inside by complete surprise. Major

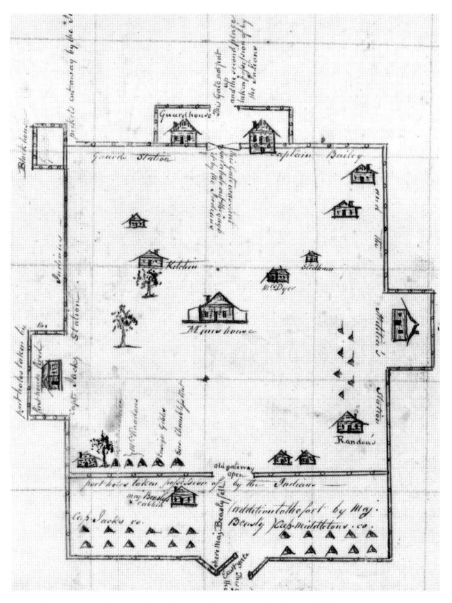

Map of Fort Mims. *Courtesy of the Alabama Department of Archives and History.*

Beasley became one of the first casualties of the battle when he was struck down as he desperately tried to close the fort's open eastern gate. The occupants of Fort Mims were nearly overwhelmed and forced to flee to the interior structures of the fort to organize a defense. They finally managed to stem the initial Red Stick onslaught, but the attackers launched a second assault, which spelled doom for the fort. In the massacre that followed, Fort Mims was destroyed, and the great majority of those in it were killed. Only a handful of those in the fort, no more than thirty, managed to make a desperate escape. The Red Sticks had won a stunning and complete victory.

Genuine fear swept throughout the Southwest frontier regarding what the strike portended for American settlements. In few places was that fear more pronounced than in the Natchez area in the western Mississippi Territory, which, even by that time, was still the economic, cultural and population center of the territory. Though Natchez was far removed from the scene of the fighting, rumors ran wild that the area had also been targeted by Natives. During this brief "Mississippi Panic," runners were sent from town to town in the region, advising settlers to seek shelter. A small number of temporary stockades, similar to those in the Tensaw region, were hastily thrown up for the safety of groups of these refugees from an imagined combined Creek and Choctaw advance. Closer to the area where actual fighting raged, in Wayne County, a mere sixty miles or so from Mims, at least two forts were established around the community of Winchester. Farther north, near modern-day Columbus, at Plymouth Bluff on the Tombigbee River, Fort Smith was also erected.

Official plans for reprisal were quickly put in motion. Armies from the Mississippi Territory, Tennessee and Georgia would simultaneously converge on Red Stick territory from different directions. Besides engaging Red Stick forces, these troops would also burn villages and crops and other supplies, forcing the hostile Creeks to give up the fight.

The Mississippi Territory's militia, under the command of Ferdinand Claiborne, became the first army to be engaged, portions having already been involved in the fight at Fort Mims. In the fall of 1813, Claiborne's soldiers sought out Red Sticks throughout the Alabama River region, engaging in several small skirmishes and a pitched battle at a place called the Holy Ground on December 23, 1813. Claiborne's force of volunteers, militia and friendly Choctaws destroyed the town and set its defenders to flight. It was the last significant battle in that theater of the war, as the focus of attention soon turned to the east and north.

General John Floyd commanded the main Georgia army that was raised in response to the Red Stick threat. Advancing from central Georgia to the banks of the Chattahoochee on the Mississippi Territory's eastern border in the fall of 1813, Floyd's men constructed Fort Mitchell as a supply base and launched two major offensives in its attempts to subdue the Red Sticks

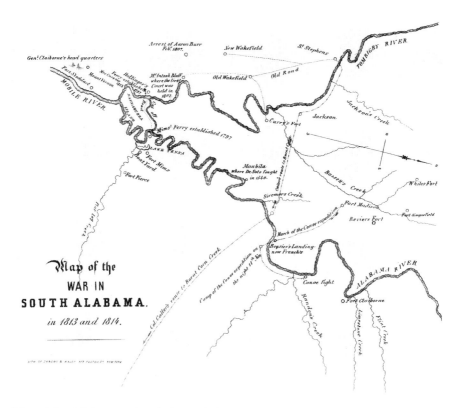

Map of Creek War campaigns in South Alabama. *Courtesy of the Alabama Department of Archives and History.*

in this theater. They destroyed the village of Autossee on November 29, 1813, killing about two hundred Red Sticks in the fighting. On January 27, 1814, as Floyd's army made its way toward another principal Creek population center, Red Stick forces fell upon it in a devastating surprise attack near Calabee Creek. Floyd's army narrowly escaped destruction before beating back the attackers and retreating to Fort Mitchell. Before they could reorganize for another expedition into enemy territory, the short-lived war was over.

The third and most consequential theater of the war featured campaigning by Tennessee volunteers and militia, regular army troops and a number of Native allies in the northeastern and central-eastern portions of the Mississippi Territory. It would be the campaigns of these armies and the leadership of Andrew Jackson that brought the war to a sudden close in the spring of 1814. Already among the foremost spokesmen for the interests of the West, Jackson saw in the massacre of Fort Mims an opportunity

Depiction of the Canoe Fight, a skirmish between territorial militiamen led by Sam Dale and Red Stick warriors in the Alabama River on November 12, 1813. *Mississippi Department of Archives and History.*

to eliminate European influence on the Gulf Coast and acquire from the Creeks valuable land for the growing country.

Jackson had already acquired a military reputation in the War of 1812. In early 1813, he led a force of Tennesseans to Natchez to take part in the defense of the Gulf Coast against a threatened British attack. His dreams of early glory were quickly dashed, however, when his men were dismissed before seeing action. Jackson swallowed his pride and led his men back to Tennessee via a long, exhausting march up the Natchez Trace back to Nashville. As Jackson had nonetheless earned the respect of his men and the acclaim of the citizens of Tennessee, his soldiers began calling him "Old Hickory" for his toughness. Jackson would soon have the opportunity to live up to that nickname and more.

After arriving back in Tennessee, Jackson was given command of one of two forces of Tennessee militia raised in response to the attack on Fort Mims. They laid waste to the Creek village of Tallushatchee on November 3, 1813, and less than a week later moved on to the village of Talladega, where Creeks allied with the United States lay besieged by Red Stick forces. Jackson's men shot down the Red Sticks in droves in the battle there on November 9. Jackson desired to continue on his path of destruction in the

Andrew Jackson. *Courtesy of the Library of Congress.*

winter but ended up spending more time trying to simply keep his army intact and supplied than plotting military strategy for the remainder of the year. When he was finally reinforced in January 1814, Jackson again took the offensive.

Jackson targeted a Red Stick force that was then gathering at the village of Tohopeka, located in a bend of the Tallapoosa. The Creeks called the one-hundred-acre plot of land Cholocco Litabixee, or "the horse's flat foot," but the Americans simply called it Horseshoe Bend. Jackson was delayed in his approach, however, by two well-planned surprise attacks. On January 22, 1814, at Emuckfau Creek and on January 24 at Enitachopco Creek, his army suffered serious setbacks inflicted by Red Stick forces, which forced him to retreat, regroup and secure additional reinforcements. With an army soon swelled to over five thousand men, Jackson headed toward Tohopeka again in March 1814, finally arriving on March 27.

At Horseshoe Bend, the American army found one thousand warriors under Menawa lying in wait behind an impressive fortification that spanned 350 yards across the neck of land in the curve of the river. The barricade consisted of logs stacked five to eight feet high and was situated in a way that subjected attackers to crossfire. Though formidable, Jackson saw that the Creeks had essentially trapped themselves behind their fortification. He dispatched General John Coffee along with his Native allies to the opposite side of the river to block their only avenue of escape and made plans for his attack.

Jackson began the decisive battle with an artillery bombardment. With the Red Sticks screaming defiance, his artillery ineffectually poured shots into their barricade. During the bombardment, Coffee and his Native allies entered the fight. Several Cherokees crossed the river and captured the Red Sticks' canoes to prevent them from being used to escape and then pressed on into the village, eventually setting it on fire. When Jackson saw the smoke from the fires of Tohopeka and realized the ineffectiveness of the artillery bombardment, he ordered an all-out frontal assault. The soldiers charged energetically and scaled the fortifications in a matter of minutes.

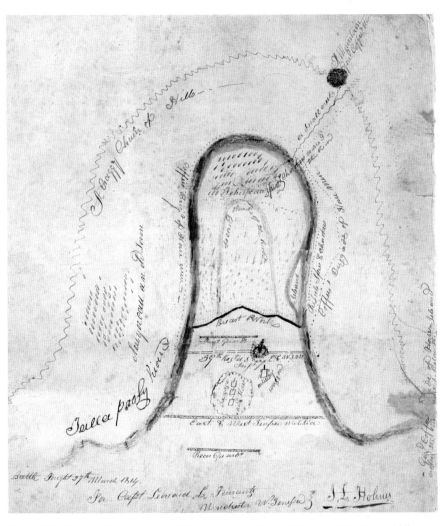

Map of the Battle of Horseshoe Bend. *Courtesy of the Alabama Department of Archives and History.*

Once the barricade had been breached, the battle turned into a slaughter in which more Natives died than in any other battle in United States history. The Red Sticks fought defiantly, but being assailed on both sides by superior numbers sealed their doom. Jackson's men counted over 550 Red Stick bodies on the field after the battle, and officers estimated the total killed to be upward of 900. Jackson's army, on the other hand, suffered less than 50 killed and about 150 wounded. Though scattered pockets of Red Stick resistance remained to be eliminated, their power had been shattered.

Tennesseans greeted Jackson as a hero on his return to Nashville. At a time when the War of 1812 had been going badly for the country, he had destroyed his enemy on the battlefield and earned the respect and admiration of the nation. On June 18, 1814, Jackson became a major general in the U.S. Army, responsible for the Seventh Military District, composed of Louisiana, Tennessee, the Mississippi Territory and the Creek Nation.

A daunting task awaited him. Secretary of War John Armstrong ordered Jackson to report to Fort Jackson and assume control of treaty negotiations with the Creek Nation. An advocate for land-hungry westerners, Jackson expected the Creeks to pay dearly for the war. Since he also wanted to prevent the Creeks from having contact with the Spanish and British, he viewed removing the Creeks from the region as a necessity to national security. Altruistically, he felt the Creek way of life was so incompatible with that of white settlers that removal was the only way for them to survive. In the end, he required the cession of twenty-three million acres of land, one-half of all Creek territory, to the United States. This land amounted to almost three-fifths of the future state of Alabama and one-fifth of Georgia. The Creeks had no choice but to sign the Treaty of Fort Jackson on August 9, 1814. Ironically, of the nearly three dozen chiefs who signed on behalf of the Creeks, only one is believed to have been a Red Stick.

The ink had not yet dried on the Treaty of Fort Jackson when Old Hickory first focused his attention on who he thought were the real instigators of war, the British and the Spanish. Jackson knew of British plans for an offensive, as well as their intention to utilize Red Sticks in the effort. He had also heard that thousands of veteran British soldiers would soon arrive from Europe to assist in operations on the coast. In late August, Jackson moved his headquarters to Mobile, closer to the developing threat, and began strengthening Fort Bowyer, located on Mobile Point, in order to better guard Mobile Bay.

Fort Bowyer constituted the primary line of defense for Mobile Bay and the city itself. On September 12, 1814, the fort survived an attack by a combined British navy and army force meant to open the way for an overland assault on New Orleans. The British had no choice but to limp back to Pensacola, which they had earlier established as their base of operations, and rethink their plan of attack.

Angered at Spanish complicity in the British offensive, Jackson planned an attack against Pensacola. Admitting in a letter to Secretary of State James Monroe, Jackson said, "I act without the orders of the government." He explained his reasons for invading Spanish Florida with confidence that the administration would eventually justify his actions. Jackson arrived

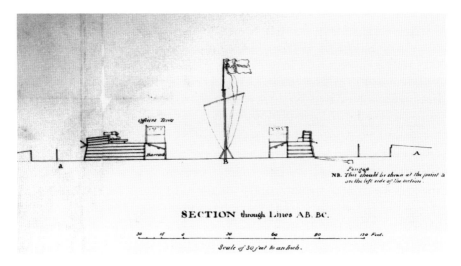

Sketch of Fort Bowyer. *Courtesy of Fort Morgan State Historic Site.*

outside of Pensacola on November 6, 1814, and, after a brief affair, gained the town's surrender in only a matter of minutes. At a cost of less than twenty casualties, Jackson had delivered a severe blow to British plans on the Gulf Coast. His mission accomplished, Jackson returned the town to Spanish authorities.[18]

Quickly learning of British intentions to attack New Orleans, Jackson next moved to counter that threat. Once there, he organized one of the most diverse forces in history to defend the city, which included local militia, a company of free Black men, some Choctaw warriors, a Mississippi Territorial cavalry unit, Tennessee and Kentucky riflemen and two U.S. Army infantry regiments. He even gathered the aid of Baratarian pirates led by Jean Laffite.

The leading elements of the British army had arrived outside of New Orleans by December 23, after brushing aside a small American naval presence at the Battle of Lake Borgne. Jackson moved to attack the intruders that night in a combined army-navy operation. Technically a draw, the battle consisted of confused fighting in darkness and fog and did little damage to either army, but it halted the British advance on New Orleans. The battle did allow Jackson's men to establish a defensive position along an old millrace known as the Rodriguez Canal, a four-foot-wide and ten-foot-deep rampart that stretched nearly three-quarters of a mile from the river into a swamp. Although neither army knew it at the time, diplomats in Europe had already drafted the treaty that would end the war. On December 24, 1814, British and American representatives signed the Treaty of Ghent. Word would not arrive on the Gulf Coast until after the looming contest for the Crescent City.

The British launched their primary fatal assault on January 8, 1815. Beginning their attack with the launch of a signal rocket, the British columns surged forward in a fog soon blown aside by the wind. Jackson's men greeted the attack with artillery and musket fire, which tore holes in British lines as they moved across the open field. In less than two hours of fighting, Jackson's army had inflicted more than 2,000 casualties on the British forces: 291 killed, 1,262 wounded and 484 captured. Jackson lost less than 20 men in one of the most surprising and lopsided victories in American military history. The British retreated back to the Gulf but made another attempt at taking Mobile, actually capturing Fort Bowyer in a second assault on that outpost on February 11, 1815, before getting word of the signing of the Treaty of Ghent.

The war's results profoundly impacted the Mississippi Territory's development. Land-hungry Americans and their enslaved laborers would soon pour into the territory to claim millions of acres of land acquired in the Treaty of Fort Jackson. The path toward statehood now seemed certain. Simultaneously, the campaigns of the War of 1812 on the Gulf Coast had allowed American forces to at last secure possession of Spanish West Florida and incorporate portions of the former colony into the Mississippi Territory. Through the remarkable victory on the plains of Chalmette, they had ended forever any European interference in regional affairs. Unprecedented numbers of settlers moving into these new lands would finally push the issue of statehood to the forefront.

4

THE GREAT MIGRATION

o early American settlers, the millions of acres of relatively cheap and
extremely productive land that lay within the Mississippi Territory
formed "the land of promise, flowing with milk and honey." Fertile,
abundant and beckoning to those eager to make their fortune, the land
that became the twentieth and twenty-second states sounded a clarion call
for thousands throughout the nation in an age when land acted as one of
the surest paths to security and wealth. As sure a form of currency as any
coin, bill or note, the land held tangible promise that could be unlocked by
anyone with the willingness to toil. Its beauty, both aesthetic and practical,
captured the attention of early settlers in a way that later generations cannot
understand. Early settlers of the Mississippi River Valley described its setting
as "inconceivably beautiful"; those who arrived in the Tennessee River Valley
were known to refer to the area as "Happy Valley"; those who settled along
the Alabama River basin raved about its productive soils as the "Acadia of
Southern America."[19]

So many settlers made their way to the Mississippi Territory between 1798
and Alabama's statehood in 1819 that its peopling is often referred to by
historians of the era as the "Great Migration." On par for its time with any
general movement of people in American history, this settlement of what
became Mississippi and Alabama is remembered as a milestone event in the
region's development, which contributed substantially to the trajectory of
both its demographic and cultural development. This settlement was part
of a larger western expansion of the United States. In 1800, there were only

The Alabama River. *Courtesy of the Library of Congress.*

two states west of the Appalachians, and they had a combined population of about 386,000. By 1820, eight new western states had been formed in the trans-Appalachian South, which over 2 million people called home. When Mississippi assumed statehood in 1817 and Alabama followed two years later, they did so as a center of growth in a dynamic new frontier of an expanding nation.

This migration occurred, to a large degree, at the expense of the area's Native populations, who were compelled to cede large tracts of their ancestral domain to the federal government during the territorial period. In a series of treaties signed between 1801 and 1816, the Choctaws, Chickasaws, Cherokees and Creeks all relinquished claim to enormous swaths of their ancestral homelands lying within the bounds of the Mississippi Territory. While they would cling to tracts of land in the region well into the statehood era, these cessions, agreed to under duress, were the beginning of a decades-long period of transformation of the region from a Native domain to an American community. And this would eventually culminate in the forced removal of Native groups in the 1830s.

So massive and sudden was American westward migration into the newly opened Mississippi Territory that in the Eastern Seaboard states of the South, especially Virginia and North Carolina, many established residents feared the depopulation would wreck their economies, ruin their political standing and permanently retard their development. It has been estimated that over two hundred thousand residents of North Carolina alone left that state for the Mississippi Valley between 1790 and 1815. Witnesses to this exodus often referred to those who ventured to the fertile lands of the Mississippi Territory as being seized with "Alabama Fever" (in reference to the river that ran through some of the best lands in the eastern section of the province) and less often "Mississippi Fever" because they were figuratively burning with a desire to have a piece of the rich new lands as soon as possible. A letter from North Carolina political leader James Graham to Tar Heel statesman Thomas Ruffin captured the simultaneous concern, wonder and disdain with which some viewed the departure of so many of their neighbors:

> *The Alabama Feaver* [sic] *rages here with great violence and has carried off vast numbers of our citizens. I am apprehensive, if it continues to spread as it has done, it will almost depopulate the country. There is no question that this feaver* [sic] *is contagious....For as soon as one neighbor visits another who has just returned from the Alabama he immediately discovers the same symptoms which are exhibited by the person who has seen the allureing* [sic] *Alabama.*[20]

Those who witnessed this movement of people through the wilderness of the Old Southwest were struck by the scale of what they saw. Their attempts to quantify the number of people and vehicles underscore their astonishment. Creek Indian Agent Benjamin Hawkins, whose agency lay along the Federal Road in central Georgia, wherein he scrupulously recorded details of what occurred in the region, reported that in one five-month span in late 1811 and early 1812, he saw 120 wagons, 80 carts, 3 carriages and exactly 3,726 people pass by as they followed the route westward. Another man, himself traveling against this tide of immigration as he ventured from the Mississippi Territory to eastern Georgia in 1816, reported that in the course of nine days, he encountered 141 wagons, 102 carts, 10 stages, 14 gigs, 2 coaches, 29 droves of cattle, 27 droves of hogs, 2 droves of sheep and an estimated 3,840 people. Even deep in the settled portions of the territory, the flow of emigrants startled established residents. A Natchez newspaper reported in 1818 that between 10 and 15 families passed by the city every day, making their way to new homes in the territory, and that these numbers were steadily increasing.

Top: Depiction of a stagecoach. *From* Forty Etchings, *by Basil Hall.*

Bottom: Stagecoach guard gun. *Courtesy of the Mississippi Department of Archives and History.*

The pace of the migration into the Mississippi Territory was startling but uneven. In 1800, the vast Mississippi Territory had a mere three relatively sparsely populated counties, with only two, Adams and Pickering, located in what would become Mississippi. These counties were located along the Mississippi River in the extreme western section of the territory and contained a population of just a little over 4,000, including enslaved people. The lone county in the eastern section of the territory, Washington, located north of Mobile along the Tombigbee River, claimed only 1,250 inhabitants. By 1810, in the middle of an initial and ultimately smaller wave of migration that started with the formation of the territory in 1798 and ended with the outbreak of the War of 1812, the counties of the western portion of the territory (which became Mississippi) claimed 31,000 residents, and the eastern (which became Alabama) claimed 9,000. At the conclusion of the brief but more dramatic second wave of migration, initiated at the conclusion of the war in 1815 and continuing until the economic uncertainty of the Panic of 1819, the state of Mississippi claimed 75,000 residents, and the state of Alabama claimed nearly 144,000. In the short span of a decade, the population of Mississippi had more than doubled, while that of Alabama had multiplied an incredible sixteen times. While settlers set up homesteads throughout the territory, three areas received the bulk of the new arrivals: the Natchez area, the lower Tombigbee River valley region and the Tennessee River Valley.

This veritable flood of humanity came primarily from other southern states and those along the Eastern Seaboard of the nation. There were notable numbers of people from Pennsylvania, Connecticut and New Jersey scattered throughout, and the Tennessee River Valley overwhelmingly became a destination for people from the state of Tennessee. In virtually every other corner of the Mississippi Territory, however, Americans from Georgia, North Carolina, Virginia and occasionally South Carolina provided the majority of new inhabitants.

Added to the influx of new arrivals seeking to legally settle were a handful of older residents who likewise held no clear title to the land on which they lived. Some operated trading establishments and had become fixtures in the areas they served. "Indian countrymen," as they were known, had settled among the Native towns years before any vestige of American authority appeared in their vicinity and established themselves in the unique niche of economic intermediary American expansion facilitated.

While most of the new immigrants arrived from elsewhere in America, a substantial number hailed from Europe. These old world settlers, who came primarily from the British Isles, with a smattering of French and Germans among them, often were fleeing the same sort of difficult economic conditions as their American-born neighbors and were similarly hoping to find their fortune in the area's rich soil. Especially prominent among these groups were Scotch emigrants, who formed closely connected small settlements in several places, such as "Old Scotch Settlement" in Jefferson County. That community was formed around 1805 by Scotch families who had first made their homes in North Carolina and Tennessee upon their arrival in America. Learning of its presence via family and friends, others followed.

The Vine and Olive Colony, established in what is now western Alabama, near the confluence of the Black Warrior and Tombigbee Rivers, is perhaps the most well-known ethnic community in the Mississippi Territory. Founded by a band of exiled veterans of Napoleon's defeated army and French refugees from a slave rebellion in Saint Domingue (Haiti), the colony came about after an 1817 grant by the U.S. Congress of some ninety thousand acres to the French Emigrant Association. It earned its unique name because of a stipulation in the grant that the settlers cultivate grapes and olives. It was a pointed attempt to make crystal clear the scheme's agricultural nature and that it was not meant to be a potential military operation that might aim to return Napoleon to power in Europe or allow him to assume power somewhere else. Although many of the grantees never made it to the banks of the Tombigbee River, choosing instead to sell their lots and settle in New Orleans or Mobile, between one hundred and two hundred French families (many actually from the French colony of Haiti and not France itself) established the town of Demopolis on the granted lands. When a survey revealed the city had been created on land just outside of the acreage granted to them, however, they abandoned that community and established the towns of Aigleville and Arcola a short distance away within the approved tract designated by Congress. Despite high hopes and the best of intentions, the colony never developed as planned. Within a decade, almost all of the original settlers had departed the area for various reasons, with the handful who stayed being swept into the tide of American settlement of the region and ultimately having lent little more than a name and a legend to the area's cultural development.

Though they had no choice in the matter, enslaved people were also a pivotal part of the migration to the Old Southwest, which would help define the social and economic development of the Mississippi Territory. While not all white settlers who moved to the territory enslaved people themselves, involuntary servitude nonetheless became central to the visions of how the land might be utilized to the best advantage by the greatest majority of the new arrivals. This only continued a trend that resulted in Mississippi's Black population doubling between 1810 and 1820 and again between 1820 and 1830. Slavery had a long history in the land that became Mississippi by the time of the migrations that populated the state in its formative era, having been part of French, Spanish, British and even Native societies, but never had it assumed so central a role on so massive a scale as it did during the first decades of the nineteenth century.

A slave coffle. *Courtesy of the Library of Congress.*

While lone travelers could be seen on the roads, migrants most often traveled in groups; frequently, one family made its way westward, but sometimes several from the same vicinity made the trip together for safety and companionship. For almost all of them, the trip was a very long one. According to one estimate, the average distance of a migration to the Mississippi Territory was around five hundred miles along haphazardly maintained trails through the wilderness. For a smaller number, the trip involved floating down one of the region's major waterways to their destination. Travelers usually departed in the fall, when the roads were generally in their best condition—hard and dry—and the numerous creeks and rivers that needed to be crossed, for the most part without the aid of bridges, were less susceptible to flooding. Caravans made their way over these routes at the rate of fifteen to twenty-five miles per day, depending on the size of the party and the conditions encountered. For most, the journey involved a few weeks of travel at minimum and at most a month or more.

The new arrivals came in almost as many forms and fashions as there were individuals. "By horse, by wagon, by boat, and by foot the flood of humanity poured in," Charles Lowery, a leading authority on the migration into the Mississippi Territory, observed. In the words of one contemporary observer, they traveled with "all their worldly possessions packed in wagons, while their women rode atop the baggage or in four-wheeled carriages or two-wheeled carts, depending on the economic status of the family." Others with less means carefully packed their possessions into hogshead barrels and rolled them mile after weary mile to their destination via mule power. Whatever cattle and hogs the immigrants laid claim to were driven along the road with them. The whole process bore the appearance of one continuous, slow-moving, discordant assemblage of men and beasts passing through the forests and fields of the region. An exceedingly small number, mostly individual travelers, occasionally stopped for the evening at one of the area's few roadside taverns, but for the overwhelming majority, their only stops were to make nightly camps, where they cooked whatever food they had and gathered around the fire for warmth and conversation before getting some sleep under the stars. They slept fitfully, for newcomers could routinely hear wolves and large cats howling in the distance and innumerable rustlings in the woods made by the region's native wildlife.[21]

Immigration involved expense and all too often endangered health. For a single man, the trip west might cost him between $100 and $200 in supplies and miscellaneous expenses; for an average family with a few enslaved laborers, the cost could be well over $1,000 at a time when most people counted themselves fortunate to earn that amount over the course of a year. Provisioning these people as their caravans creaked and groaned through the wildernesses of the Old Southwest spurred an industry unto itself among enterprising individuals in the region. Legendary figure Sam Dale, hero of the "Canoe Fight" during the Creek War of 1813–14, became one of dozens who recognized the immigrants as potential customers, contracting with some for transportation or as a guide to the Mississippi Territory from as far away as Savannah. Dale moved to provide individually a service that was much in demand by hundreds of travelers by attempting to secure food and provisions that would allow them to complete their journey. A surprising number came to the region inadequately supplied, and hundreds more came without means to obtain

Depiction of travelers on a flatboat. *Courtesy of the Library of Congress.*

necessaries even if they could be found—and with regional trading centers scattered and isolated, they commonly could not. "Bread was the first demand [of travelers]," noted Dale. "With tears, with persuasions, even with threats they demanded it. Human nature was not proof against such distress." Supplied or not, the vicissitudes of travel, exposure to the elements and lack of access to prompt or adequate medical attention could make the journey a harrowing experience. Many became sick along the way to their new home, and an unknown but substantial number perished in the process, their forgotten graves ironically lying along the now-overgrown trails that were to serve as their path to a better life.[22]

Regardless of the high hopes for the future that fueled immigration to Mississippi from elsewhere in the United States or abroad, leaving one place to make a new home in another involved a certain degree of uncertainty, a temporary upheaval and often a permanent sense of loss for early settlers. Nobody contemplating a move could know definitively what their future held. A move westward was a gamble fraught with danger and potentially disastrous consequences. Despite the seeming flood of migration the region witnessed, there were many reasons that kept countless numbers from ever making the journey, including fear of failing to find economic success, having one's health compromised due to rugged conditions on the frontier or simply being unable to leave loved ones.

Sam Dale. *Courtesy of the Mississippi Department of Archives and History.*

Family units formed the core of the wave of settlement that washed over the Mississippi Territory. Often, two or more households of close kin traveled together. While some households made the trip west as a unit, many came in two or more waves, frequently delineated by generation, with the first serving as scouts to locate suitable tracts of land for the rest. Still, immigration tore family groups apart. Visits to relatives would thereafter be infrequent and very difficult; for many leaving for the Mississippi Territory, it would be the last time they saw some family members. Realizing this, at best, tempered the excitement of a fresh start and, at worst, consumed the thoughts of some immigrants with dread. Women especially seemed to fear migration because of the ways separation from familiar surroundings particularly affected them. Many contemplated with perfect horror attempting to raise children alone in the wilderness without the networks of support and companionship friends and family provided. Of course, for the enslaved people who accompanied many early settlers, the sense of irreversible separation proved even more real. Heartrending farewells took place in slave quarters as families prepared to start for the west, at which time tearful goodbyes were exchanged among the extended nuclear family who made up the only home most slaves knew. In an era in which enslaved people rarely had a chance to travel beyond the borders of their home county, much less to another region of the country, migration must have been viewed by them with an even greater sense of finality.

The process of legally establishing claim to this luxuriant land would prove more complicated than many would have dreamed. Swaths of the Mississippi Territory had been claimed alternately by France, Spain, England and even the State of Georgia, and each had issued titles to portions of its lands over time. This conflicting, overlapping tangle of existing deeds yielded tremendous confusion over legal ownership of land in the state that would occupy both territorial and state courts for decades. Many early

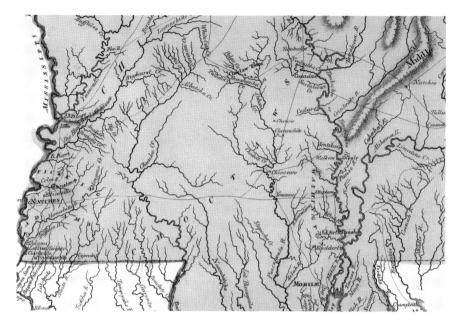

Opposite: Surveyor's compass. *Courtesy of the Mississippi Department of Archives and History.*

Above: Detail of a map of the Mississippi Territory in 1816, showing its developing road network as areas were settled. *Courtesy of the David Rumsey Map Collection.*

arrivals simply squatted on their lands of choice until professional surveys and organized auctions could take place. It has been reported that when Mississippi achieved statehood, there were more intruders, or illegal settlers, than legal residents in some counties. When public land sales finally did take place, it was not uncommon for illegal squatters to attend and intimidate or otherwise threaten those who might wish to legally purchase the land on which they resided.

Land offices located east of the Pearl River, in Washington County, and west of that river, in Adams County, handled the bulk of the land sales in the early territorial years. Later, an office opened in Nashville, Tennessee, and subsequently moved to Huntsville to serve the territory's northern reaches after the end of the Creek War. These administrative centers were to sell at auction in an orderly fashion all unclaimed lands to which Native title had been extinguished. They did a booming business in executing their charge, handling the sale of hundreds of thousands of acres of the Mississippi Territory in a mounting torrent of activity over the decade and a half prior to statehood.

In any discussion of the settlement of the Mississippi Territory, it is important to keep in mind the fundamentally transitory nature with which settlers commonly viewed the homesteads and communities they founded. The people who comprised the Great Migration commonly continued their movement after their arrival in what became Mississippi and Alabama, either moving elsewhere in the region or continuing their journey farther west soon after, constantly in search of better land and more promising opportunities. "Few persons in this country consider themselves fixed," noted one resident at the time, "hence the motives to making solid improvements…and forming those kindly relations which constitute the main charm of social life, operate but feeble here. This accounts for the general unembellished condition of the country." Regardless of how long they stayed, residents of the Mississippi Territory turned their attentions toward establishing a home and making a living immediately upon arrival.[23]

5

LIFE ON THE FRONTIER

The people who settled the Mississippi Territory lived on a rugged frontier where literally just about everything had to be built, created or grown from scratch. True pioneers, their early settlements form the beginnings of many of the communities that populate maps of the region today. Their experiences in settling the land, building their homes and carving out farms from the landscape represent one of the essential stories from the territorial period.

Once they arrived at the spot they intended to live on, settlers immediately set to work constructing housing for themselves and their family, commonly a single-room log cabin. They first felled trees by axe, cut them into the appropriately sized logs by saw and notched them with an adz to fit together like so many puzzle pieces. Then, sometimes assisted by neighbors—if they had any—they rolled them into place, and the frame took shape. They attached a roof of barked slabs, laid like shingles, and applied clay chinking to gaps between the log walls to keep out the elements. Eventually, many of these early homes would have split clapboards for siding as they were added to or otherwise modified. Furnishings inside these early homes could be extremely sparse. Countless numbers of early Mississippi Territory homes featured only a scattering of the humblest homemade furniture, with a few iron pots, an assortment of glazed crockery and gourds equipping the kitchen. Puncheon floors partially covered with animal skins were a common sight. Virtually every home contained a rifle, a vital tool for obtaining meat that could of course be used for defense and, not infrequently, sheer

The John Looney House, a two-story dogtrot cabin in St. Clair County, Alabama. *Courtesy of Creative Commons.*

entertainment. Tallow candles, oil lamps or sometimes the fireplace alone lit their dim interiors. Just about anything else settlers needed they made by hand, from clothing and quilts to tools.

Mississippi Territory residents were generally well-fed, even if their meals were of limited variety. Meat from both wild and domesticated animals formed the centerpiece of the early settler diet, with many residents filling their pots with a variety of plentiful game. Deer, turkey, geese and an assortment of freshwater fish frequently graced dinner plates in settler homes. Corn served as the staff of life in the territory, however, and one of the first tasks when setting up a new homestead involved clearing a patch of land for its cultivation. Many residents of the territory ate corn virtually every day—off the cob, in mush, ground into meal and baked into varieties of cornbread. The list of the other most commonly available vegetables included turnips, okra, peas and sweet potatoes.

The people seated around territorial dinner tables would have been dressed plainly, many in homemade clothes. Simple dresses, homespun trousers, white cotton shirts and hunting shirts predominated, especially in the earliest years of the territory. Ubiquitous in the early territorial years, hunting shirts, loose-fitting, rugged, all-season frocks and the accompanying buckskin leggings were inspired by Native dress. Early American settlers borrowed more than just clothing styles from their Native neighbors, especially learning to appreciate many staples of the Native diet and how to prepare and store certain foods. Some even consulted their Native neighbors for medical advice when family members became sick, tapping into the extensive Native knowledge of medicinal plants.

The Mississippi Territory's residents spent the great majority of their time and energy trying to earn a living. The huge swaths of open lands made available to American settlers in the Mississippi Territory happened to be suited perfectly to open-range grazing, and a substantial number of settlers pursued herding as an avocation. Surveyor Andrew Ellicott noted that he found "the cattle in the settlement of Natchez…are extremely numerous, and it is not uncommon for the wealthy planters to possess from one to two hundred head and sometimes more." Claims filed for damages during the Creek War of 1813–14 reveal widespread herding activity among small farmers during the territorial days, as numerous claimants had the largest portion of their wealth tied up in cattle and hogs. In roundups that sound more like something out of the American West than the Gulf South, herds were routinely collected in temporary pens, fattened with corn and branded before being driven long distances into trading centers for purchase.[24]

The cultivation of cotton was the most lucrative enterprise in the territory, and by the time of statehood, it had become entrenched in the regional economy. While yeomen farmers throughout the area could be found growing small plots of the fiber, large planters settled the area's fertile river valleys early on and ushered in the plantation-style agriculture that would, within a generation, define much of the antebellum South's economy. Hence, much of territory's developing economic system would literally be built on the backs of enslaved Black Americans. Regardless of what masters might publicly say or want to believe about the system of bondage they engaged in, they knew the enslaved were not satisfied with their station. Even early in the territorial years, Governor David Holmes confided in a letter, "Scarcely a day passes without my receiving some information relative to the designs of those people [slaves] to insurrect." Actual events provided more than enough fuel to stoke the fire of hysteria, for masters were keenly aware of famous slave rebellions, such as the German Coast Uprising near New Orleans (1811). Fear sparked repressive measures to keep the enslaved population under control, much of it codified into law in the first state constitutions of Mississippi and Alabama.[25]

Above: Cotton field in Alabama. *Courtesy of Clay Williams.*

Opposite, top: Enslaved people picking cotton. *Courtesy of the Library of Congress.*

Opposite, bottom: Oxen yokes were used by frontier settlers when working pairs of animals. *Courtesy of the Mississippi Department of Archives and History.*

While numerous details of the lives of enslaved people varied from location to location, their experiences generally followed certain contours regionwide regarding basic work patterns, housing, food and medical care. Enslaved people customarily worked six days a week in the Mississippi Territory, with Saturdays often being a half day of work at certain times of the year. Workdays commonly began at or before daylight and ended at dark. Everyone had a task; children as young as five might be charged with carrying water to older enslaved people in the fields, while elderly enslaved people might help prepare food. Depending on each enslaver's prerogative, a few holidays might allow for all work to be halted; Christmas

Day was observed nearly universally in this manner, but at some plantations, Independence Day and New Year's Day were celebrated as well. Food for the enslaved was generally abundant, if not varied, with rations of corn meal, salt pork and molasses nearly ubiquitous and flour, rice, peas, meal and, on occasion, other meats being provided. Enslaved people usually lived in humble, sparsely furnished wooden cabins, almost invariably with no floors and often no daubing between the split timber logs. Owners or local physicians who made periodic visits to plantations provided what medical care the enslaved people needed outside of the herbal remedies composed within the slave quarters. The authority of enslavers was absolute, and every aspect of life for the enslaved lay circumscribed by their owner's prerogative. Perceiving no other recourse for relief from their situation, many enslaved people ran away. It is difficult to find any issue of a major newspaper in the territorial and early statehood years without a mention of runaway enslaved people.

That the enslaved population managed to endure their situation can, to a large degree, be credited to the concepts of family they fostered and maintained, even if many relationships within it were fictive, and this became a vital organizing force in the enslaved community. Enslaved people recognized aunts, uncles and other extended kin, creating a community within a community that promoted a sense of belonging and helped organize a social network which gave a degree of stability and control that was utterly lacking outside of the slave quarters.

Regardless of race, territory residents were part of a rough-edged frontier society. The first judge of the Superior Court of the Mississippi Territory, Ephraim Kirby, left us with a colorful, if unflattering, description of his impression of the general population of the region to which he had been sent in 1804. He observed that the area had long been the refuge of criminals and assorted outlaws who deemed it beyond the reach of legal authorities or, in Kirby's words, those "who prefer voluntary exile to the punishments ordained by law." He went on to provide a sweeping indictment of the frontier culture he encountered by declaring:

> *The present inhabitants (with few exceptions) are illiterate, wild and savage, of depraved morals, unworthy of public confidence or private esteem; litigious, disunited, and knowing each other, universally distrustful of each other.—The administration of justice, imbecile and corrupt. The militia, without discipline or competent officers.*[26]

Kirby's judgment may have been a harsh overgeneralization, but it contained an element of truth worthy of notice by anyone attempting to understand life in the Mississippi Territory. The region developed on the fringes of a more established American society, and as a consequence of its location and circumstance, it virtually encouraged a rowdy, self-reliant and insular culture. Mississippi and Alabama were as much Western as Southern during their formative era, and their territorial years define their transition from unchartered frontier to the heart of the Deep South.

Family stood at the center of frontier life in the Mississippi Territory. Many households contained large extended families, with grandmothers and grandfathers, on occasion, but more commonly aunts, uncles, cousins, nieces and other especially beloved friends. These family groups frequently formed close-knit quasi-independent communities that provided mutual assistance with everything from socialization and education to child rearing.

Life on the frontier was inherently precarious. Crude living conditions and limited medical knowledge, primary among several factors, combined to make life expectancies much shorter in the territorial years than they are today. The suddenness with which illness, often mysterious in origin, could strike and debilitate its victims kept people on edge. Various and vaguely described "fevers" or "agues" carried away people on a regular basis and were a near-constant threat to health. Others were suddenly stricken with "paralytical shocks," "consumption" and a host of other illnesses that, in short order, sent them to their graves. Families with multiple children almost invariably lost one to sickness before the age of five, and mothers passed away during childbirth at an alarming rate. Epidemic diseases periodically swept through the region and carried off dozens and sometimes hundreds at a time. The foremost among these, yellow fever, proved particularly devastating. "Yellow jack," as it was known, is a viral disease spread by mosquitoes. No cure existed at the time. Many of those who contracted the dreaded illness died within a matter of days—sometimes even hours. The fever usually struck in the late summer or early fall in the years it made an appearance. The closely packed riverside population and trading center of Natchez proved to be a perfect host and experienced some of the deadliest outbreaks in the territory.

Home and natural remedies, superstition and the kindness of loved ones provided the only defenses against illness for most. Herbs, extracts from roots and poultices derived from certain plants commonly sufficed as frontier medicine, and good diets and moderation regarding alcohol and tobacco were advised as preventative measures for a host of troubles. For just

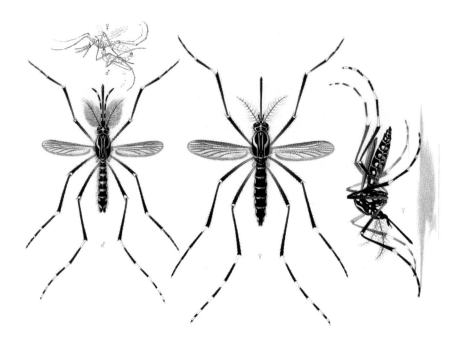

Above: The *Aedes aegypti* mosquito, transmitter of yellow fever. *From* Os Mosquitos no Pará, *by E.A. Goeldi.*

Opposite: The first newspaper published in what became Alabama, the *Mobile Centinel*, May 30, 1811. *Courtesy of the Alabama Department of Archives and History.*

about anything beyond the scope of these treatment methods, a sick person might be "bled," the widespread belief being that imbalances and impurities in the circulatory system were at the root of many maladies and could be addressed only through the purging of blood.

Opportunities for learning were fundamental to the stability and nurturance of territorial society, but the slow growth of both demonstrates the raw frontier nature of the region at the time. Precious little was done prior to statehood toward the establishment of schools, and those who did receive any educational instruction often did so through private tutors. The territorial legislature, in 1802, established Mississippi's first institution of higher education, Jefferson College (named in honor of President Thomas Jefferson), but it took nearly a decade before the school actually opened.

Those interested in intellectual enterprises nonetheless found outlets in a number of private organizations that devoted themselves to the study of literature and science and advancement of educational institutions.

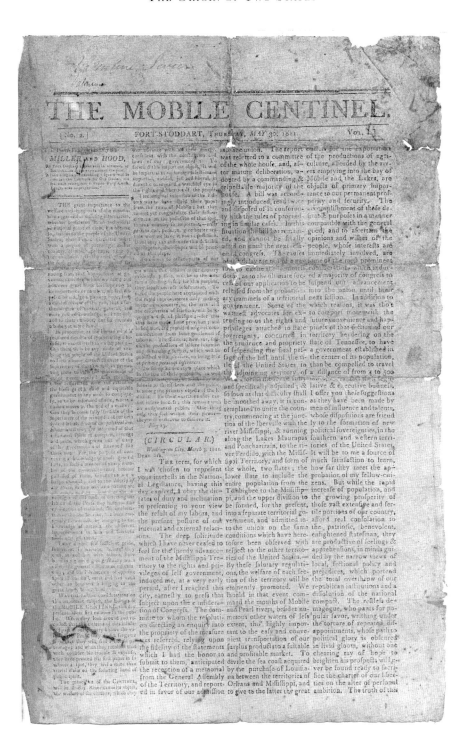

THE MOBILE CENTINEL.

[No. 2.]   FORT-STODDART, THURSDAY, MAY 30, 1811.   Vol. I.]

MILLER AND HOOD,

(CIRCULAR.)

Washington City, March 3, 1811.

DEAR SIR,

The Natchez region proved to be the hotspot for such organizations. The Mississippi Society for the Acquirement and Dissemination of Useful Knowledge, the Franklin Society, the Natchez Mechanical Society and a Literary and Library Company were examples of the type of organizations that celebrated academic pursuits in the pre-statehood era along the banks of the Mississippi.

While Mississippi and Alabama eventually became firmly established parts of the "Bible Belt" in the South, religious institutions traversed a difficult road toward becoming a major influence in their societies during the territorial years. By some estimates, as few as one in twenty Mississippians belonged to any church at the time of statehood, and religious institutions of the era in general played as little a role in the life of citizens of the state as they did at any point in the state's history. Among the first and most influential expressions of any newfound religious fervor in the Mississippi Territory were camp meetings. A frontier phenomenon that persisted throughout the antebellum period and beyond in the South, these assemblies had their origins in 1700s England but acquired their distinct American form in the fields and forests of the Old Southwest. Physically, camp meetings were gatherings of hundreds of people in wilderness clearings, assembled to hear gospel preaching by traveling ministers. They often lasted for several weeks at a time and customarily occurred in the fall. They were commonly the largest events to occur in many of the isolated frontier communities in the Mississippi Territory and quickly became among the region's premier social events. These rural gatherings had an electric effect on the spread of religion in the territory, and from them, some of Mississippi and Alabama's most prominent Christian churches and organizations can trace their roots.

Three evangelical Christian denominations—Baptist, Methodist and Presbyterian—captured the hearts and minds of the majority of those who affiliated themselves with any church during the frontier period. Baptist congregations were meeting clandestinely in the Natchez area as early as the 1780s, and by 1800, there were four in the Mississippi Territory; there were eighteen in 1813, and nearly forty at the time of Mississippi's statehood. Presbyterians first moved to establish themselves in the Mississippi Territory with the appointment of missionary James Hall in the Natchez area in 1800. Several preaching "stations" were established through his efforts and furthered by those who followed him. The Mississippi Territory's first presbytery, consisting of several early congregations that grew out of the first missionary-established stations, formed in 1816. The Methodist Church became the largest religious organization in the territory. The Methodist

Depiction of a frontier camp meeting. *Courtesy of the Library of Congress.*

message struck a popular middle ground among a cross-section of the lower- and middle-class population, as they were regarded neither as poor as the Baptists or as well off as the Presbyterians. The first Methodist missionary in the territory, Tobias Gibson, arrived in Natchez in 1799 and organized the first Methodist church there a year later. By 1816, Methodists had formed an independent local conference.

Few aspects of the territorial period witnessed as much change as its developing transportation network. At the time of the Mississippi Territory's organization, a few scattered wilderness roads traversed its interior, and virtually all economic activity was confined to a few key ports along the major waterways that connected the region with the Atlantic. The recorded experiences of those who attempted to travel any substantial distance overland seem filled with trials to the point of being almost comical. "I have had occasion to say a great deal about roads," commented one traveler who traversed a territorial period road in what had been the eastern Mississippi Territory. "But I pronounce that along which our route lay on the present occasion, to be positively, comparatively, and superlatively, the *very worst* I have ever traveled in the whole course of my peregrinations." The writer referred specifically to a section of the Federal Road in the eastern section of the territory, but he might have been speaking about any number of roads on the southwestern frontier.[27]

At the time of the Mississippi Territory's formation, it could take as long for mail to travel from the nation's capital in Philadelphia to Natchez as it would for that same mail to travel from Philadelphia to Europe. By the early 1800s, overland mail delivery time between Washington, D.C., and the Crescent City—traveling through the Mississippi Territory—had been reduced to a mere twenty days with multiple deliveries per week. The territorial hinterlands off this main corridor, however, could remain out of touch for extended periods. Even the regionally important commercial, transportation and population center of St. Stephens, located north of Mobile, for example, received mail only once per month as late as 1816. The poor road system likewise restricted overland trade until well into the statehood era, when the lucrative profits promised by cotton crops grown in the interior finally spurred significant private financial investment in road creation and improvement.

A few major transportation routes handled most of the long-distance traffic in Mississippi's early years. The Gaines Trace, connecting the Tennessee and Tombigbee River valleys and presaging the modern Tennessee-Tombigbee Waterway System in the territory's northern reaches, was opened by its namesake, George Strothers Gaines, in 1810. In the southern section of the territory, the Natchez–Fort Stephens Road and an assortment of other east–west paths that generally connected the Mississippi and Tombigbee River valleys, today often collectively

Section of the original route of the Natchez Trace. *Photograph by Clay Williams.*

remembered as the apocryphal "Three Chopped Way," remained vital transportation corridors throughout the territorial period and beyond. The Federal Road was opened in 1806 as a postal route connecting Georgia and the Mobile area, but within a few short years, it became a primary route for immigration into the eastern section of the territory.

One road, though, the famed Natchez Trace, looms especially large in our memory of the era. The road is now commemorated as a 444-mile-long national park roughly following the original route. During the territorial years, it connected Natchez and Nashville, but it traces its origins to a time when neither city existed. True work on improving the road to something more than a wilderness footpath, at the time known variously as the "Path to the Choctaw Nation" or the "Chickasaw Trace," began in 1802. At the height of its use prior to the War of 1812, the Natchez Trace served as a primary route of travel and communication between the lower Mississippi River valley, the Midwest and the eastern United States. It existed, for the most part, as a one-way route, however. Thousands of traders who had traveled with the current down the Ohio, Tennessee and Mississippi Rivers aboard flatboats laden with goods to be marketed in Natchez and New Orleans used the route for their return home. Several other less-celebrated trade and transportation routes were hacked out of the fields and forests of the Mississippi Territory, especially after the War of 1812, when the pace of settlement increased, connecting the new communities that were being founded throughout its borders. Even if these routes were primitive by modern standards, taken together, they revealed the territory to be a growing and thriving place, as developed as any state in the region.

6

THE ROAD TO STATEHOOD

By 1817, the Mississippi Territory had been in existence for nineteen years, by far the longest territorial period experienced by any state to date. Its recent growth seemed to assure imminent statehood, but the manner in which it would enter the Union remained a point of great contention. Would the territory become one state or two? Where would the border be drawn if it were divided? Where would its center(s) of government be located in either scenario? A pervasive east–west sectional rivalry would play a key role in deciding how all of those and more questions would be answered.

Prior to the Creek War, the Mississippi Territory contained only two widely separated pockets of substantial American settlement. Natchez ranked as the only true city in the entire territory for many years, its orderly grid of streets and numerous brick buildings along the Mississippi riverfront virtually unique in the region until well into the 1810s. The city and its environs served as the capital of political, cultural and economic life in the western section of the territory. The area of American settlement along the rivers immediately north of Mobile gradually assumed a similar, if less centralized, position in the east. While this area contained no major towns, it featured the only other significant concentration of American settlements for a period.

The physical distance between these two areas of settlement and the imbalance in their influence and prestige fueled an early animosity. As early as 1803, a mere five years after its creation, settlers in the lower Tombigbee

River region requested Congress divide the Mississippi Territory. They observed that as things stood, the nearest center of law lay hundreds of miles away, "all of which distance is a howling wilderness with its usual inhabitants of Savages and beasts of prey." As a result, communication with the territorial government routinely proved difficult and sometimes impossible. The only practical result of this initial effort was the creation of a new judicial district for the Tombigbee region. The issue festered among the eastern section inhabitants in the ensuing years. Eastern section residents—meaning virtually anyone outside of the Natchez District—only grew more estranged from the more populous and affluent Mississippi River settlements as time progressed. Leaders in the Natchez area, on the other hand, were keenly aware of the economic and political dominance of their region in the territory's affairs and desired to see it enter the Union as a single state, with Natchez remaining its capital.[28]

Efforts to move the territory toward statehood prior to the War of 1812, led by congressional delegates George Poindexter and William Lattimore, had been stymied by this internal squabbling. The territory's unwieldy size worked against their efforts as well, since, in the words of a Senate committee report drafted after a review of one proposal for statehood, it stood "disproportionate to the size of any of the largest states which now compose our confederation." To the north of the territory's original northern boundary, all the land stretching to the Tennessee state line and from the Mississippi River in the west and the Georgia border in the east had been added to its jurisdiction in 1804 once the State of Georgia relinquished all claim to that area. Further complicating matters was the fact that, owing to the terms of the agreement in which Georgia gave up those claims, statehood for the Mississippi Territory technically required that state's approval. When the War of 1812 and associated Creek War broke out, all efforts toward statehood were temporarily put on hold.[29]

The war years, nonetheless, were marked by significant events that would ultimately bear tremendous influence on the arrangement of future state borders. Just to the south of the Mississippi Territory's pre-1812 border and to the east of the Orleans Territory (the forerunner of the state of Louisiana, established 1804) lay the Spanish colony of West Florida. Americans had long desired to acquire the gulf borderland, through which most of the area's major rivers flowed, and the federal government even claimed it via a controversial understanding of borders described in the Louisiana Purchase. Following a successful rebellion against Spanish authorities in Baton Rouge in 1810, the Madison administration hastily annexed a portion of the colony into its control as part of the Orleans Territory. On March 5, 1812, Congress approved the admission of the Orleans Territory into the Union as the state of Louisiana, with statehood becoming official on April 30. In May, the United States asserted jurisdiction of the section of the colony stretching between the Pearl and the Perdido Rivers. The only problem was that Spain continued to garrison troops in Mobile, and no American officials could bring into actuality their nation's assertion of control of the region without risking a potential altercation.

In February 1813, Secretary of War Armstrong ordered General James H. Wilkinson to at last take formal possession of Mobile through military force. Wilkinson arrived in April with some six hundred men and several gunboats, with an additional four hundred troops from Fort Stoddert set to join him. He demanded the Spanish leave what he boldly proclaimed to be the territory of the United States. Fort Charlotte commander Layento Perez, outnumbered, outgunned and with no promise of support forthcoming, surrendered without a fight on April 13. It would be the only territorial acquisition made by the United States during the War of 1812, and the land Spain surrendered was quickly incorporated into the Mississippi Territory. In the meantime, Georgia had officially given its long-awaited approval for the formation of a state or states from its former claims in the Mississippi Territory in January 1813. The path for statehood seemed clear.

As a result of the treaty that ended the Creek War, millions of acres of choice agricultural lands were ceded by the defeated Creeks to the federal government. Officials immediately put plans in motion for them to be opened to American settlement. Hoping to capitalize on the situation and the potential to more heavily influence any new state of which they were to be a part by virtue of a certain regional population boom, many eastern section residents soon began to evaluate the benefits that might fall to them should the territory be admitted as one state. Some of those in the western section, however, fearing the future diminishment of their economic and political influence the cession forbode, similarly began to countenance division. They could not help but note that nearly three-quarters of Native claims to lands in the eastern section of the territory had been extinguished, and the area would soon be flooded with American settlers, while a majority of lands in the western section remained legally in the possession of Native groups and were hence not available for American settlement. A switching of the longstanding imbalance in population and wealth between the eastern and western sections of the Mississippi Territory appeared on the immediate horizon.

The U.S. House of Representatives, at length, took up the issue of statehood for the Mississippi Territory once again in February 1815, as it had continued to receive more memorials from the territorial legislature and private citizens asking for consideration of their concerns. While many Southern congressmen were anxious to see the admission of an additional state (or states) and the political spoils its representation might entail, many northern and eastern political leaders were of course hesitant for the same reason. Seemingly impassable divisions of opinion over the issue of statehood were as deep as they had ever been in 1816, and no clear path toward statehood appeared in sight.

Taking matters into their own hands, influential citizens from the eastern section of the territory in October 1816 called a special meeting at the home of prominent minister and government official John Ford, along the Pearl River in Marion County, to determine how they might most effectively push the issue of statehood forward. Seventeen delegates from fifteen of the Mississippi Territory's twenty counties met in this "Pearl River Convention" between October 29 and October 31, 1816. Not surprisingly, the assembly overwhelmingly consisted of eastern section residents and its agenda to recommend action favorable to that section was clear to all. While a majority of territorial counties were represented, those western counties that were notably absent from the gathering contained well over half the population and wealth of the Mississippi Territory as a whole. Regardless of this inconvenient fact, the "Convention of the Delegates of Several Counties of the Mississippi Territory" drafted a memorial to Congress pointing out the inefficiency and inexpediency of dividing the territory on practical, legal, economic and political grounds. Neither side would meet the population requirements for statehood soon, if ever, according to their calculations. They also called attention to a host of other concerns mitigating against division, including that the territory bordered a foreign country, that Georgia had agreed to forming a state from its former claims as soon as possible and that forming one state was inherently more economical that creating two. Gauging the direction of the political winds in Washington, they pointed out that a large Southern state might "counteract the imposing influence of the large northern and middle states." The convention also sent Superior Court Judge for the Tombigbee District Harry Toulmin, one of the most influential political leaders in the eastern section of the territory, to Washington, D.C., to represent its interests.[30]

Delegate William Lattimore's persistent efforts to have the territory divided since the end of the Creek War clearly had found traction by the time of Toulmin's arrival. A wearied Congress had long prior made up its mind to follow the original recommendation for division, which had been set out in the 1812 Senate report for the sake of both simplicity and geographic equity. On March 1, 1817, Congress approved, and President James Madison signed the Enabling Act that granted admission to the Union of the western section of the territory as the state of Mississippi. It approved an act creating the Alabama Territory from the eastern section on March 3, 1817, with a provision that the territorial government it authorized become effective as soon as Mississippi formed a constitution and state government. In other words, should Mississippi fail in that regard, Alabama's statehood was in jeopardy as well.

As the line of division of the territory seemed to suit no one, that technicality was no small issue. Barely had the ink dried on the Enabling Act before eastern section residents asked for a revision of the line, while in the west, prominent officials, including Poindexter and fiery political leader Cowles Mead, expressed disbelief that Lattimore had allowed Mobile to be given to the Alabama Territory and threatened to have the entire matter brought before Congress again. Both eastern and western section residents clamored to have the entirety of the Tombigbee basin in their respective states, and its arbitrary division by federal officials set off a wave of grumbling on both sides of the prospective border. In the end, the majority of Mississippi Territory citizens, in the east and west, in effect agreed to compromise on the compromise, realizing that further fighting would only delay admission to the Union.

The line Congress suggested remains the boundary of the states of Mississippi and Alabama today with one minor change. The boundary, as authorized by Congress, began at the Gulf of Mexico about ten miles east of Pascagoula, ran north to the northwest corner of the boundary of Washington County, then moved gently northeastward to the point where Bear Creek emptied into the Tennessee River and then went along that river to the Tennessee state line. In the 1819 congressional act authorizing the Alabama Territory to form a state government, officials ordered the lower border be redrawn to run slightly southeast from the northwest corner of Washington County, Alabama, to the Gulf of Mexico, as surveyors determined the original north–south line had infringed slightly on the eastern borders of Wayne, Greene and Jackson Counties in Mississippi.

Mississippi's Constitutional Convention gathered on July 7, 1817, in a Methodist church on the grounds of Jefferson College in Washington. Meeting for six weeks during the height of a hot and humid summer,

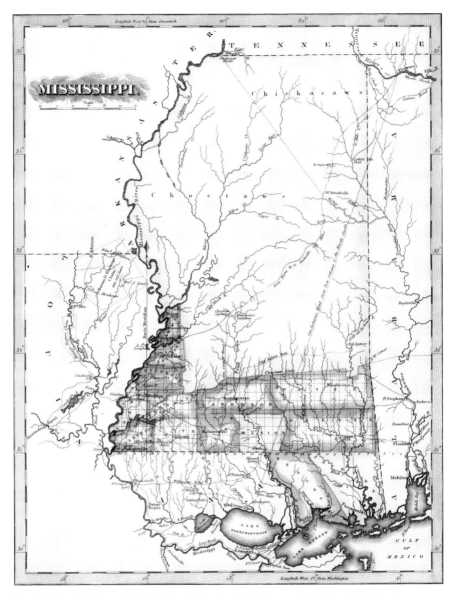

Detail of an 1822 map of Mississippi, showing the Alabama-Mississippi state border. *Courtesy of the David Rumsey Map Collection.*

the convention's forty-seven delegates representing Mississippi's fourteen counties (one did not attend) assisted in hammering out the document by which the new state would be governed. Their backgrounds indicated affluence—twenty-one had served in the general assembly and thirty-one were either lawyers, planters or both—and the constitution they adopted was a decidedly conservative document. While it granted voting rights to all white men who had lived in the state for a year (and their voting district for six months), it also required they pay state or county taxes or have served in the militia. In line with other state constitutions written at the time, it had a bill of rights guaranteed to state citizens. In response to the longstanding contempt for the perceived excessive authority that had resided within the territorial executive office, the convention clearly established the legislative branch, directly responsible to the voters, as the most powerful branch of state government. Further, it made the offices of governor and lieutenant governor elected directly by the people. The convention attempted to address persistent complaints of inadequacies within the territorial judiciary by creating new and independent court systems. The constitution also carried provisions allowing the legislature to pass laws pertaining to manumission of enslaved people and requiring enslavers to treat their chattel humanely. Virtually all the language pertaining to the protection of the enslaved *allowed* legislation to that end to be drafted at some future date; the new constitution clearly set out the institution of slavery as a fundamental part of the new state's social and economic structure. It gave only lip service to support for education and left the amendment process largely in the hands of the legislature alone instead of the citizenry. Highlighting the cultural environment in which the delegates lived, a motion to include a provision

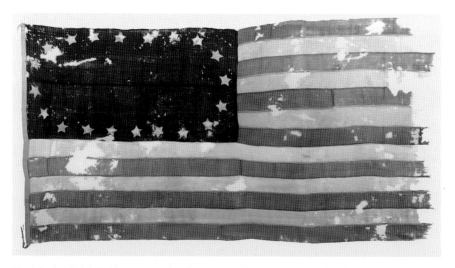

Twenty-star flag. *Courtesy of the Mississippi Department of Archives and History.*

outlawing dueling sparked much debate but, in the end, failed to garner enough votes to pass.

The convention adopted the constitution on August 12, 1817, and forty-five of the forty-seven attending delegates signed the document on August 15. On cue, a cannon placed just outside the doors of the convention hall boomed a salute to announce the moment. The constitution did not undergo scrutiny by the voters, but rather, the convention sent it directly to Washington for federal approval. The Senate passed its approval on December 3, and the House passed it on December 8. President James Monroe signed the act admitting Mississippi as the twentieth state on December 10, 1817. David Holmes, the last territorial governor and president of the constitutional convention, was named the first governor of the new state, while Walter Leake and Thomas Hill Williams took their seats in the U.S. Senate and the venerable George Poindexter took his in the House. Mississippi's long, tortuous road toward statehood had come to an end.

The act creating the Alabama Territory called for elected officials representing the area in the Mississippi Territory's general assembly to serve the remainder of their terms as members of Alabama's first governing body. President James Monroe appointed William Wyatt Bibb, a trained doctor, veteran politician and recent but well-connected arrival in Alabama, as governor of the new Alabama Territory. St. Stephens was designated as the territorial legislature's meeting place. On January 19, 1818, fourteen legislators gathered there at the Douglas Hotel for the Alabama Territory's inaugural legislative session. Thirteen of those present held membership in the legislature's lower house; only one councilor from the body's upper house, James Titus, attended. In this and a second session held in November, the Alabama Territory General Assembly established the inner workings of government and organized basic services for its citizenry. The legislature passed a flurry of laws in a matter of weeks, including the chartering of Alabama's first school (St. Stephens Academy) and bank (Tombeckbe) and the naming of Creek Indian Agent John Crowell to represent Alabama as its delegate in the

William Wyatt Bibb. *Courtesy of the Alabama Department of Archives and History.*

nation's capital. The assembly also organized over a dozen new counties in the land it administered in the course of its proceedings.

None of the dozens of statutes the general assembly considered in those first two sessions involved quite as much energy or passion as the debate over the selection of a future state capital. St. Stephens, located in the extreme southwest of the territory, clearly would be replaced as the seat of government once statehood was achieved. But since the designation of a new capital city would mean a great deal of prestige, influence and coveted economic activity in whichever region it was located, the battle for that title starkly exposed the new mounting rivalry between North (meaning the Tennessee Valley) and South Alabama (meaning the virtual remainder). While almost every corner of the Alabama Territory belatedly featured rapid growth, the pace of development in North Alabama proved truly exceptional. In the fall of 1818, Madison County alone laid claim to approximately one-sixth of the territory's entire population and accounted for about one-quarter of all taxes paid into its treasury. Neighboring Tennessee Valley counties also had sizeable and swiftly growing populations that, in sheer numbers and pace of development, as a group outstripped almost every area to their south.

Fully aware of Alabama's population dynamics, the commission that was formed to find a centrally located site for the state capital recommended Tuscaloosa as a compromise between North and South Alabama. During the interim between meetings of the legislature in the summer of 1818, however, Governor Bibb had been busy working to establish a capital farther south at the junction of the Cahaba and Alabama Rivers, where he envisioned a great city. Tapping connections in Washington, he obtained federal grants of land for the scheme and, in his address delivered to the legislature at the opening of its inaugural session, revealed his plan for Alabama's future capital. In sealing the deal, South Alabama legislators made several concessions to their counterparts in North Alabama, who sought to leverage their larger population to fullest advantage in return for allowing the future state's seat of government to be located along the Cahaba. They directed that Huntsville would serve temporarily as the state capital until facilities in the planned city of Cahawba could actually be built—something far from certain in the eyes of many—and only if the still-imaginary town remained the capital in 1825 could it be declared permanent.

Early in 1819, the matter of statehood for Alabama came up for discussion in Congress, spurred on by powerful friends such as Georgia Senator Charles Tait and the informed lobbying of local leaders, such as John W. Walker. In a particularly resonant petition sent during the Alabama Territory's final

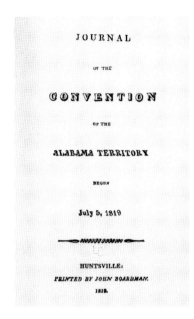

JOURNAL

OF THE

CONVENTION

OF THE

ALABAMA TERRITORY

BEGUN

July 5, 1819

HUNTSVILLE:
PRINTED BY JOHN BOARDMAN.
1819.

Front page of the journal of the
Alabama Constitutional Convention.
Courtesy of the Library of Congress.

legislative session, for example, Walker reminded Congress of the wave of immigration washing over the region and that, with a population of nearly seventy thousand (white) people, the Alabama Territory easily surpassed the population of Mississippi and compared favorably to other recently admitted states. With Tait's guidance, the statehood bill at last cleared Congress, and on March 2, 1819, President James Monroe signed the act that enabled the formation of a government for the state of Alabama. Elections were to be held in May to choose delegates to a constitutional convention scheduled for July.

Alabama's constitutional convention opened in a vacant cabinet shop in Huntsville on July 5, 1819. Forty-four delegates representing the territory's twenty-two counties—eight of them from host Madison County—attended. It ranked as a distinguished group by frontier standards; from the convention would come several of the future state's governors, judges of its supreme court, senators and even a vice president of the United States (William Rufus de Vane King). The convention's members took their business seriously and immediately set to work creating a subcommittee of fifteen to draft the constitution, and they busied themselves with the body's housekeeping and numerous other smaller associated matters that demanded attention. Working six days a week throughout July, they soon had a completed document that the convention approved and signed on August 2, 1819.

The constitution proved a relatively liberal governing instrument for the time, broadly reflecting the interests of the new state's significant yeomen farmer population and exhibiting a special understanding of Alabama's frontier nature. It called for universal adult white male suffrage, with no property, taxpayer status or militia service qualifications. Requirements for holding office were likewise minimal, the framers having eschewed traditional property qualifications. Acknowledging a fact of life in a state undergoing a dramatic increase in population, the constitution stipulated

Above: Reconstruction of the building in which Alabama's Constitutional Convention was held in Alabama Constitution Hall Park, Huntsville, Alabama. *Photograph by Mike Bunn.*

Opposite: James Monroe. *Courtesy of the Library of Congress.*

short periods of residency for candidates for office. The constitution called for the popular election of judges rather than their appointment, included a bill of rights, established a state-owned bank and detailed specific measures for the advancement of education, such as the dedication of a section of land in every township for that purpose and establishment of a state university. Although Alabama's governing document expressly sanctioned the institution of human enslavement, it encouraged humane treatment of bondsmen by owners, guaranteed enslaved people some limited fundamental rights and set specific criteria for emancipation. Per their instructions, the framers sent their constitution directly to Congress, not to the people of Alabama, for approval. The end of Alabama's protracted territorial experience, now approaching its twenty-first anniversary, finally appeared in sight.

Alabama's state legislature opened its first session on October 25, 1819, in Huntsville. Over the course of the next seven weeks, the body passed some seventy-seven acts designed to bring the constitution into practical effect. The legislative acts passed ranged from routine matters, such as setting the salaries of state officials, to a rather aspirational appropriation for an engineering survey to determine the best way to connect—ostensibly via canal—the Tennessee and Mobile River systems. The legislature established

a court system, outlined rules and regulations for the establishment of a state militia and codified procedures for the establishment of a means to patrol the enslaved population. It also organized a taxation structure that relied, in large part, on assessments of various forms of property to provide the revenue necessary for the government's operation. Mindful as ever to balance political spoils among North and South Alabama, legislators chose John W. Walker of Huntsville and William Rufus de Vane King of Selma as the state's first United States senators. As the general assembly prepared to bring its proceedings to a close in mid-December, the congressional resolution to admit Alabama into the Union finally came to President Monroe's desk in Washington. He signed it on December 14, 1819, and Alabama officially became the twenty-second state of the United States of America.

AFTERWORD

Mississippi and Alabama's transformation from Old Southwest frontier to the heart of the Old South proved remarkably swift. In the span of a mere generation, the two states that were formed from the Mississippi Territory emerged as vital centers of the Deep South's growing economic might, political power and cultural development. Everything about their ascendancy on the national scene could be traced to their shared territorial experience.

Between 1820 and 1860—during what is now widely known as the antebellum period in regional history—Mississippi and Alabama became the epicenter of a distinctive Southern society. Both witnessed an unprecedented concentration of wealth in the hands of a minority of citizens, enabled by the rise of the institution of slavery, which was employed in the production of cotton. This agricultural might, in turn, was made possible by the acquisition of millions of acres of land that originally lay in the hands of Native groups. The removal of Native occupants and the settling of their ancestral lands by Americans and thousands of enslaved laborers of African ancestry are perhaps the seminal themes in a shared pattern of development that brought both states into their own as major players on the American scene. The result of both of these trends was that, by any measure, Mississippi and Alabama were transformed from struggling frontier economies into powerhouses of agricultural trade in the decades prior to the Civil War. Millions of dollars' worth of exports, largely in the form of bales of cotton, were shipped out of the region to domestic and international ports stretching from New York to

London and beyond during the era. This trade became so much a part of regional finances that even those not directly connected with the institution of slavery or the production of cotton were inextricably linked to both.

Likewise, Mississippi and Alabama came into their own as bastions of national political power in the decades prior to the attempted dissolution of the Union. Andrew Jackson, of course, would propel himself into two terms as the nation's chief executive in large part based on his military accomplishments in the region. And he came to personify the interests of the people of the region. But Mississippi and Alabama each assumed their own degree of influence in the years between 1820 and 1860, a fact perhaps best communicated by the fact that when secession did occur, the first capital of the Confederacy was located in Montgomery, and Mississippi politician Jefferson Davis was chosen as the nation's first president. As important as either their economic or political rise in our understanding of Mississippi and Alabama's development in the decades after being admitted to the Union is the fact that the states were also at the heart of the cultural maturation of the region. Their distinctive cultural environment, as it regarded everything from religion and race relations to tastes in architecture, were in every respect at the heart of the Old South experience. All of these characteristics contain stories of persistence, accomplishment, innovation and leadership that are worthy of celebration. Yet at the same time, they also contain stories of bigotry, hatred, inequity and failure that are justly condemned. In this regard, the stories of Mississippi and Alabama seem to be the very epitome of Southern history in many ways. Indeed, the region's response to defeat in the Civil War, its rejection of Reconstruction, its long reliance on agriculture, reluctant modernization and its infamous troubled racial history are all long-running themes not only in Mississippi and Alabama but also in Southern history, which can be, in various ways, connected to their shared foundational era.

Today, Mississippi and Alabama contain populations in the millions, with large cities like Jackson, Mobile, Montgomery, Birmingham and Huntsville—any one of which would have dwarfed the entirety of the Mississippi Territory's population at its founding. Both have developed into thriving, modern states that have gone to great lengths to shed the persistent stigma associated with the more regretful aspects of their common past. Yet in so doing, both have come to appreciate more than ever the importance of understanding their formative era as a shared origin story. The Mississippi Territory is where Mississippi and Alabama—and in no small part the story of the Deep South as a unique part of the American saga—began. It is difficult indeed to contemplate what they are today and how they might develop in the future without comprehending how they began. For this and many other reasons, the territorial period in Mississippi and Alabama history continues to resonate for all of those with an interest in the past, present and future of this special region.

BIOGRAPHIES

John Adams

Second president of the United States John Adams held office from 1797 to 1801, at the time of the Mississippi Territory's creation. He appointed some of its first officials, including Governor Winthrop Sargent. Adams County, one of the first two counties created in the territory, was named in his honor.

William Wyatt Bibb

William Wyatt Bibb served as the first governor of the Alabama Territory, being appointed to the position by President James Monroe upon the division of the Mississippi Territory. Previously, Bibb served in the state legislature of Georgia and in both the U.S. Congress and Senate. Bibb won the election to become the state of Alabama's first governor in 1819 but died after an extended illness in July 1820. He is best remembered in Alabama history for his plan to locate the new state's capital in Cahawba, a town created for the purpose, rather than in an existing centrally located community as recommended by the territorial legislature. He is buried in a small cemetery in Coosada, where his plantation once stood. Bibb County, Alabama, is named in his honor.

ISAAC BRIGGS

Isaac Briggs was appointed as the surveyor general of the Mississippi Territory in 1803. A Pennsylvania native and a devout Quaker, Briggs studied at the College of Pennsylvania before moving to Maryland and embarking on a distinguished career as an engineer and surveyor. He helped Andrew Ellicott lay out the boundaries of the District of Columbia in the 1790s, was awarded a patent for a steam engine in 1807 and worked on a variety of projects of national note, such as the Erie Canal and the James River and Kanawha Canal. At the behest of his personal friend Thomas Jefferson, he traveled, in 1804, to what became the route of the Federal Road across Georgia and the Mississippi Territory, making important notes and astronomical observations along the way that would prove invaluable in later developing the route.

PETER BRYAN BRUIN

One of the first three judges appointed to serve the Mississippi Territory in 1798, Peter Bryan Bruin was the only one to reside in the territory at the time. Bruin, a Revolutionary War veteran, moved to the Natchez District from Virginia in the 1780s while it was still under the control of Spain. Several other families joined him in making the move at the invitation of Spanish authorities, and the community they established along Bayou Pierre (modern Port Gibson) became known as Bruinsburg. Bruin served as a territorial judge until 1809, afterward retiring to a life as a planter. Lake Bruin, Louisiana, across the Mississippi River from Bruinsburg, where he owned a plantation, is named after him.

AARON BURR

Aaron Burr was a prominent American politician. He served as vice president under Thomas Jefferson, but his career was decimated after he shot and killed Alexander Hamilton in this nation's most famous duel in 1804. Burr's visit to the Mississippi Territory in 1807 caused considerable unrest, as he was widely believed to be involved in a scheme aimed at capturing

Spanish possessions west of the Mississippi River and/or separating areas of the Southwest from the rest of the union. When General James Wilkinson ordered his arrest, Burr voluntarily surrendered to territorial authorities in exchange for a guarantee he would be tried in Mississippi. A grand jury in Washington found insufficient evidence to indict him on treason and allowed him to leave. Burr was later arrested and held prisoner near Mobile and eventually stood trial in Richmond, where he was acquitted in a landmark verdict that set the precedent for trials involving treason.

FERDINAND L. CLAIBORNE

Ferdinand Claiborne commanded the Mississippi Territorial militia during the Creek War and the War of 1812. Brother to Territorial Governor W.C.C. Claiborne and father to famed historian J.F.H. Claiborne, Claiborne served two terms in the Mississippi territorial legislature, getting embroiled in the political factionalism of the day. Claiborne led the first organized offensive into hostile Red Stick territory after the fall of Fort Mims, culminating in the destruction of the Holy Ground, a sacred Red Stick Native village. Suffering from poor health, he retired to his home in Natchez after the campaign. He died there in 1815.

WILLIAM CHARLES COLE CLAIBORNE

A rapidly rising politician, William C.C. Claiborne became Mississippi's second territorial governor. A Tennessee Supreme Court justice at age twenty-one and a U.S. congressman at age twenty-five, he was instrumental in pushing the Mississippi Territory into the second stage of government, which allowed for a legislative assembly. Thomas Jefferson later appointed him governor of the Mississippi Territory, where he sought to establish stability after a tumultuous beginning under the previous administration. He joined James Wilkinson in accepting the transfer of Louisiana to the United States following the Louisiana Purchase. He served as governor of the Territory of Orleans prior to becoming the governor of the state in 1812, and he served there during the New Orleans campaign of the War of 1812. After the conflict, he served briefly in the U.S. Senate until his death in 1817. Claiborne was originally buried at St. Louis Cemetery Number 1 in New Orleans but was later reinterred in the Metairie Cemetery. Claiborne Parish, Louisiana, and Claiborne Counties in Tennessee and Mississippi are named in his honor.

DANIEL CLARK SR.

A native of Ireland and officer in the British army in America, Daniel Clark Sr. migrated to the Natchez area in the 1760s while it was still a British colony. He established a large plantation on a land grant he had obtained from governmental authorities and became a wealthy planter engaged in tobacco cultivation. During the unrest, as the area transitioned from Spanish to American control pursuant to the terms of the Treaty of San Lorenzo (1795), Clark served on the "Permanent Committee" of Natchez area citizens supporting Andrew Ellicott's efforts to establish American authority in the region. Mississippi Territory Governor Winthrop Sargent appointed him a district commander in the territorial militia shortly after his arrival. Clark died about 1800. The community of Clarksville, near Fort Adams, now a ghost town but one of the few American communities of any size in the Mississippi Territory in its first few years of existence, was named in his honor.

JOHN COFFEE

A close friend and trusted subordinate of Andrew Jackson, John Coffee served with him throughout the Creek War and War of 1812, ending the war with the rank of brigadier general. After the war, he worked as a surveyor, laying out the new boundaries of the Creek Nation as described by the Treaty of Fort Jackson before being appointed as surveyor general of the northern district of the Mississippi Territory. After the creation of the Alabama Territory, Coffee helped organize a land company, which developed the town of Florence, Alabama. He lived on a nearby plantation for the remainder of his life, working as the state of Alabama's public surveyor, staying active in real estate business and being appointed by the federal government on several occasions to help negotiate treaties with the

Chickasaws and Cherokees. He died in 1833 and was buried in Coffee Cemetery in Florence, Alabama. Counties in Alabama and Tennessee are named in his honor, as are the communities of Coffeeville in Alabama and Mississippi, Coffee Springs in Alabama and Fort Coffee in Oklahoma. He is also remembered in the name of the John Coffee Memorial Bridge over the Tennessee River on the Natchez Trace parkway.

SAMUEL DALE

One of the most celebrated American heroes of the Creek War, Sam Dale was a witness to Tecumseh's famous speech at Tuckabatchee in 1811 and a participant in the Battle of Burnt Corn Creek and the campaign against the Holy Ground. He is most famous for his role in the Canoe Fight, in which he and two others killed nine Red Stick warriors in the Alabama River. He later served in the Alabama legislature and subsequently spent his last years in Mississippi. Dale County, Alabama, and the community of Daleville, Mississippi, are named in his honor. (His gravesite, marked by a memorial to him and his accomplishments, is at the Sam Dale Historical Site, located just off Highway 39, north of Meridian, Mississippi.)

SILAS DINSMOOR

New Hampshire native Silas Dinsmoor served as the official U.S. agent to the Choctaw from 1801 to 1813. Previously, he had worked in a similar capacity among the Cherokees. Dinsmoor's duties included helping keep the peace between the tribe and the American settlers of the Mississippi Territory, removing illegal settlers from Choctaw lands and encouraging the tribe to take up row crop farming. He was instrumental in arranging the Treaty of Mt. Dexter (1805), in which Choctaws ceded over four million acres of land in the southern portion of the Mississippi Territory to the United States. Dinsmoor is often mentioned in histories of the era as much for his running feud with Andrew Jackson as his work among the Choctaw. In 1811, he tried to force all people transporting enslaved people over the Natchez Trace to produce papers proving ownership in response to reports of runaways along the route. An enraged Jackson refused to comply and threatened to shoot Dinsmoor and destroy his agency. Jackson's complaints about Dinsmoor to federal officials played a role in his replacement as the Choctaw agent. Dinsmoor lived in the Mobile area afterward before retiring to Kentucky.

WILLIAM DUNBAR

Scottish-born William Dunbar immigrated to America in 1771. Arriving first in Philadelphia, he, by 1773, had found his way to the Mississippi Valley, where he became a prosperous planter by the time of the Revolutionary War. He went on to become one of the most accomplished scientists in early America, in addition to being a businessman working as an inventor, surveyor, botanist, zoologist, astronomer, mathematician and explorer who later became a member of the American Philosophical Society and a personal friend of Thomas Jefferson. He died in 1810 and was buried on the grounds of his plantation home, The Forest. A historic marker explaining his significance stands on Highway 61 near the intersection of Forest Plantation Road south of Natchez.

William Dunbar. *Courtesy of the Library of Congress.*

ANDREW ELLICOTT

Andrew Ellicott was a skilled surveyor turned diplomat. His surveying accomplishments include helping survey the famous Mason-Dixon line, establishing boundaries between Georgia and North Carolina and Ohio and Pennsylvania, laying out the national capital in Washington, D.C., and planning the city of Erie, Pennsylvania. He even became the first person to measure Niagara Falls. After the signing of the Treaty of San Lorenzo in October 1795, he was sent to Natchez to mark the all-important thirty-first parallel, which became boundary between Spanish Florida and the United States. A strong proponent of American expansion, he pressed Spanish authorities on conducting the survey, heightening tensions when he raised the American flag in town. After a year of distress, intrigue and near revolt, the Spanish eventually evacuated, and Ellicott commenced his survey, which took nearly two years.

John Floyd

Planter, politician and military officer John Floyd led the largest Georgia army raised for service in the Creek War. In the fall of 1813, he established a base of supply at Fort Mitchell, located on the Mississippi Territory's eastern border. In the winter of 1813–14, he led his troops on two expeditions into Red Stick territory, which resulted in the Battles of Autossee and Calabee Creek. Later, in one of the last actions of the War of 1812, he was sent to defend Savannah from an anticipated British assault. Floyd County, Georgia, is named in his honor.

Vicente Folch y Juan

Juan Vicente Folch y Juan served as the governor of the colony of West Florida from June 1796 to March 1811. Turmoil along the American border characterized much of Folch's administration, as he was forced to try to maintain Spain's tenuous hold on the region, despite insufficient resources. Only by swift action and promises of cooperation with American officials after the West Florida rebellion of 1810 was he able to forestall the seizure of additional portions of the colony. The Spanish government recalled Folch in 1811, and he continued his career as a military and government official in Cuba until his death in 1829.

John Ford

Methodist minister John Ford moved to the Mississippi Territory from his native South Carolina, where he served in that state's legislature, around 1810. After short stays in the areas of Huntsville and Natchez, he eventually settled with several members of his extended family along the Pearl River, just north of what is now the Louisiana boundary. There, he became a prominent and wealthy local leader. The 1816 Pearl River Convention, gathered to discuss whether the territory should move toward statehood as one or two states, met at his home. Ford represented Marion County at the 1817 Mississippi Constitutional Convention, where he served on the committee that drafted the document.

THOMAS FREEMAN

As surveyor of public lands south of the state of Tennessee, Thomas Freeman oversaw the surveying of a large portion of the eastern section of the Mississippi Territory. Prior to his work in the territory, he had helped lay out the city of Washington, D.C., surveyed various boundaries with Native lands and led an expedition of exploration along the Red River. He is most well-known for his work in the Tennessee Valley of what became the state of Alabama, where he established the Huntsville Meridian. The line would become important in surveying all public lands in the northern area of the state. He is buried in Huntsville's Maple Hill Cemetery, where a modern monument marks his grave.

EDMUND P. GAINES

Edmund P. Gaines. *Courtesy of the Library of Congress.*

During his long and distinguished career, Edmund P. Gaines figured prominently in numerous events in the Mississippi Territory and surrounding region. A Virginia native and Revolutionary War veteran, Gaines moved to the area after stays in North Carolina and Tennessee. In 1801, he was assigned to work on improving the Natchez Trace, and in 1806, he was given command of Fort Stoddert, near what was at the time the American border with Spanish Florida. Gaines placed Aaron Burr under arrest in 1807 and had him transported from Fort Stoddert to Richmond for trial. He led troops in the War of 1812 fighting along the Canadian border, returning to the South in 1816, where he worked to keep order at various posts in the greater Gulf region from Georgia to Texas for the next two decades. He died in 1849 and was buried in Mobile's historic Church Street Graveyard. Cities in Florida, Georgia and Texas are named in his honor, as were forts along the Chattahoochee River in Georgia and on Dauphin Island at the entrance to Mobile Bay.

GEORGE S. GAINES

The younger brother of Edmund P. Gaines, George S. Gaines served as an agent to the Choctaws in the eastern section of the Mississippi Territory prior to its division. Before and after the Creek War, he operated agencies at St. Stephens and on Factory Creek in what is now west Alabama. During the Creek War, Gaines proved instrumental in securing the support of the Choctaws and Chickasaws in lending military aid to the American armies in the campaigns against Red Stick Creeks in the Mississippi Territory. Later, during the process of removal of the Choctaws to lands reserved for them in the West, he contracted with the federal government to help provide assistance and supplies and coordinate the move. He remained prominent in regional affairs for several decades, becoming involved in railroading and farming in Alabama in his later years. He died in 1873 at his plantation in State Line, Mississippi, and was buried there.

MANUEL GAYOSO DE LEMOS

Manuel Gayoso de Lemos was the most famous Spanish ruler of Natchez. Arriving in 1789, he oversaw the creation and development of the town and initiated policies to entice settlers to the region. He achieved success in transforming the town from an isolated military post, and his congenial personality charmed most Natchez residents. Spain's hold on the region, however, was tenuous, and its leaders gave up the territory in the Treaty of San Lorenzo in 1795. Gayoso and other colonial officials hoped to nullify the treaty and offered excuses for not immediately evacuating, angering many American officials, including Andrew Ellicott. Gayoso eventually assumed a promotion in New Orleans when he became governor-general of Louisiana and West Florida. He died there of yellow fever in 1799. He was buried at St. Louis Cathedral in New Orleans.

CARLOS GRAND PRÉ

Carlos Louis Boucher de Grand Pré served as governor of the Baton Rouge District of the colony of West Florida from 1799 to 1808. Born in New Orleans, Grand Pré commanded Spanish posts in Louisiana and West Florida and served as lieutenant governor of the Red River District prior to his assignment at Baton Rouge. During his administration of the district, mounting tensions with Americans along the Mississippi Territory border surfaced. In 1804, a group of would-be revolutionaries led by the Kemper brothers attempted to capture him and cause a rebellion in West Florida but were unsuccessful. Grand Pré died in Cuba in 1809.

ABNER GREEN

Abner Green was the first treasurer of the Mississippi Territory, appointed in 1802 by Governor W.C.C. Claiborne and serving until he was removed in 1807 by Governor Robert Williams. A prominent local planter and political official, he also served as a justice of the peace for Adams County. Green had been involved in affairs in the Natchez region for many years prior to the establishment of the Mississippi Territory. During the short-lived Bourbon County (1785–1788), an attempt by the State of Georgia to assert control of its claims to land bordering the Mississippi River while the area lay in Spanish hands, which existed only on paper, he was appointed to serve as its register of probate.

ISAAC GUION

Isaac Guion led American forces in the Natchez District following the Treaty of San Lorenzo. He tried to establish peace during the tumultuous period prior to Spanish withdrawal as the region's various factions vied for political power. He directed much of his ire toward Andrew Ellicott, whom he believed was most responsible for the intrigue and discord. He died in 1823 and was buried in Natchez City Cemetery.

Lyman Harding

Massachusetts native and lawyer Lyman Harding arrived in Natchez on a flatboat shortly after its formation. He enjoyed a successful career in the handling of land transactions, and through his success in that line of work, he was able to become wealthy in the cotton trade. He became the state of Mississippi's first attorney general when it reached statehood in 1817. He died in 1820 and was buried in Natchez City Cemetery. His home, Auburn, is both a Mississippi and National Historic Landmark.

Carlos de Hault de Lassus

Carlos de Hault de Lassus held the position of governor of the District of Baton Rouge at the time of the West Florida Rebellion in 1810. Born in France and a veteran of the French Revolutionary Wars, de Lassus served in a variety of posts in Spanish colonial holdings in North America prior to being sent to West Florida. De Lassus tried to head off the mounting discontent of American expatriates in the Baton Rouge District through negotiation and military force, but he did not have the resources needed to put down the revolt. He was briefly held as a prisoner after the takeover of the region by rebels and retired after his release. He died in 1843 in New Orleans and was buried in St. Louis Cemetery Number One.

Benjamin Hawkins

President George Washington appointed Benjamin Hawkins as principal temporary agent for Indian affairs south of the Ohio River in 1796. He held the position until his death, becoming one of the most influential men in the Deep South during the era. From his agency on the Flint River in

Benjamin Hawkins. *Courtesy of the North Carolina Department of Archives and History.*

Georgia, he oversaw the administration of the federal government's program of "civilization" aimed at helping the Creeks become yeoman farmers and thus, in theory, more compatible with white society. Because of his position, Hawkins also became a key diplomat in disputes within the Creek Nation and those involving Creeks and white settlers. He tried hard to avert the Creek War, urging the rejection of Tecumseh's appeal to the Creeks and ordering the Red Sticks who murdered white settlers be brought to justice. He was greatly disheartened to see the conflict escalate into full-scale war with the United States and looked for ways to peacefully end the war as it raged. He was appointed as one of the initial commissioners charged with negotiating a treaty ending the war with the Red Sticks but was later replaced by Andrew Jackson. He died in Georgia in 1816. Hawkins was buried in Taylor County in a cemetery on Benjamin Hawkins Road, just off State Highway 128. A memorial to him stands in the center of the town of Roberta, Georgia. The city of Hawkinsville, Georgia, is named in his honor.

GOVERNOR DAVID HOLMES

David Holmes served as the last governor of the Mississippi Territory. His tenure helped end a long period of bitter political factionalism. He governed during the Creek War and War of 1812 and during the drive for statehood. He served as the president of Mississippi's first constitutional convention and eventually as the new state's first governor. His eleven years and one month tenure as the territorial and state governor ranks second among Mississippi's chief executives. He died in his native Virginia in 1832. Holmes County, Mississippi, is named in his honor.

ABIJAH HUNT

One of the wealthiest men in the early years of the Mississippi Territory, Abijah Hunt is most often remembered for being killed in a duel with political rival George Poindexter in 1811. Hunt, a native of New Jersey, had settled near Old Greenville (Jefferson County) after a brief but successful career as a merchant in Ohio. In the Mississippi Territory, he acquired a fortune quickly by growing, ginning and brokering cotton. In less than a decade, he became one of the largest landholders and slaveholders in the region, and he operated general stores in the area as well. He served for a brief time as a deputy postmaster in the territory and cofounded the Bank of Mississippi in 1809. Following a series of altercations with Poindexter, who was affiliated with the Democratic-Republican Party, Hunt, an outspoken Federalist, accepted a challenge to a duel. The affair took place on June 8, 1811, along the banks of the Mississippi River opposite Natchez. Hunt received a mortal wound from a shot fired by Poindexter, which he alleged had been fired early. He died hours later.

ANTHONY HUTCHINS

A British officer during the French and Indian War, Anthony Hutchins eventually settled in the Natchez District in the 1770s. He opposed James Willing's raid by American forces in the area during the American Revolution and took part in the uprising against the Spanish after they took over the region during the same conflict. He became a major political player in the United States gaining control of the area due to the Treaty of San Lorenzo. He first clashed with Andrew Ellicott and the ensuing Permanent Committee, which became the de facto governing body during the interim period between Spanish and American rule. His opposition continued against autocratic Territorial Governor Winthrop Sargent. He died in 1804.

ANDREW JACKSON

Born into humble circumstances, Andrew Jackson eventually became the greatest spokesman for the interest of the American West, a victorious military general and president of the United States. Serving as major general of the Tennessee militia, he led several campaigns during the Creek War. As much as any other single factor, his rugged determination and incredible willpower contributed to the Red Stick defeat. After securing millions of acres of Creek land for the United States via the Treaty of Fort Jackson, Jackson turned his attention to the nation's European threats. He first captured Pensacola from the Spanish and then later won one of this country's greatest military victories at the Battle of New Orleans. He served as the primary negotiator in the Treaty of Doak's Stand, where the Choctaws ceded millions of acres of land, leading the capital of Mississippi to be moved to a city named in his honor. These successes eventually catapulted Old Hickory to the White House, where he served two terms. Multiple cities and counties are named in his honor.

THOMAS JEFFERSON

Third president of the United States (1801–1809) Thomas Jefferson held office during an important period of development of the Mississippi Territory. Jefferson appointed two territorial governors and numerous other ranking officials during his term. Jefferson County, Mississippi, originally known as Pickering County, was renamed in 1802 in his honor.

REUBEN KEMPER

Reuben Kemper moved to Spanish West Florida from his native Virginia with his brothers, Nathan and Samuel, around 1800. After being forced out of the colony by authorities for extralegal activities, the Kempers settled in the Mississippi Territory, near the border village of Pinckneyville. In 1804, they attempted unsuccessfully to overthrow the Spanish government of West Florida and were captured a short time later. Reuben played a prominent role in the West Florida rebellion of 1810 and worked diligently—but again unsuccessfully—to rally support for the short-lived republic in the Mobile area. He would later fight with American forces at the Battle of New Orleans. Kemper died in Natchez in 1827. Kemper County, Mississippi, is named in honor of Kemper and his brothers.

DAVID KER

President Thomas Jefferson appointed David Ker as a judge in the Mississippi Territory in 1802. A native of Ireland, Ker had enjoyed a distinguished career as a Presbyterian minister and educator prior to his arrival in the territory around 1801. He had been the first professor at the University of North Carolina when it opened in 1795 and had directed an academy in the city of Lumberton in that state while studying law. He served as a sheriff and clerk of court in Adams County prior to assuming the office of judge. He is also credited with organizing the territory's first public school for girls in Natchez. Ker died in 1805 and was buried in Natchez City Cemetery.

WILLIAM LATTIMORE

Trained as a physician, William Lattimore served several terms as a delegate to Congress from the Mississippi Territory. He favored splitting the territory into two states for the main reason that this resolution would produce four Southern senators, as compared to only two. He died in 1843 and was buried in Lea Cemetery in Amite County, Mississippi.

WALTER LEAKE

Mississippi's third governor (1822–1825), Walter Leake, was a Revolutionary War veteran and served in the Virginia legislature prior to being appointed as a judge in the Mississippi Territory in 1807. He represented Claiborne County at the constitutional convention of 1817 and later served as one of the state's first two United States senators. Leake County and Leakesville, the county seat of Greene County, are named in his honor.

JAMES MADISON

Hailed as the "father of the Constitution," James Madison also served as the fourth president of the United States. Extremely dissatisfied with the Articles of Confederation, he was one of the principal writers of the Constitution and the Bill of Rights and was one of the authors of the famous *Federalist Papers*, which advocated for the Constitution's passage. As president, he led the United States into war with Great Britain. He also signed the Enabling Act in March 1817 that allowed for the admission of the western part of the Mississippi Territory as the state of Mississippi and organized the eastern portion as the Alabama Territory.

ANDREW MARSCHALK

Andrew Marschalk was a pioneer in Mississippi journalism. Serving in the military on the frontier at Walnut Hills (Vicksburg), he printed "The Galley Slave," the first printed piece to be published in Mississippi. He later printed the first laws of the Mississippi Territory and eventually started *The Mississippi Herald* in 1802, starting a career in newspapers that would last over thirty years. His involvement with partisan press embroiled him in many controversies, including a well-known feud with Mississippi politician George Poindexter. He died in 1838 and was buried in Natchez City Cemetery. A historic marker commemorating his role in early Mississippi history stands at the intersection of Franklin and North Wall Streets in Natchez.

GEORGE MATTHEWS

A Revolutionary War veteran, former congressman and two-term governor in the state of Georgia, George Matthews almost became the first governor of the Mississippi Territory. President John Adams nominated Matthews for the post, but the political backlash it sparked forced him to reconsider. Matthews had recently fallen out of favor at the time due to his involvement in the infamous Yazoo Land Frauds, the corruption-stained attempt by Georgia legislators to dispose of western lands claimed by the state. Matthews ended up moving to the Mississippi Territory nevertheless, and there, he married wealthy widow Mary Carpenter near Natchez in 1804. He served as a special agent of President James Madison in attempts to annex Spanish East and West Florida in his later years. He died in Washington, D.C., in 1812.

COWLES MEAD

Cowles Mead was an administrator and legislator who served the Mississippi Territory. When serving as territorial secretary, Mead had Aaron Burr arrested during the famous politician's controversial visit to the region while Governor Robert Williams was in North Carolina. When Williams returned, he reprimanded Mead for his actions, setting off a long political dispute between the two men. Mead later served in the legislature and as a delegate to the constitutional convention. He strongly opposed splitting the territory into two states and failed in his motion to name the new state Washington. He continued to serve the state but failed in numerous attempts to hold statewide office. He eventually moved to Clinton, where he became a member of the Board of Hampstead Academy (now Mississippi College). Meadville, the seat of Franklin County, Mississippi, is named in his honor.

MENAWA

Menawa led Red Stick forces at the Battle of Horseshoe Bend. Though he was wounded multiple times, he became one of the few Red Sticks to escape the battlefield. After the Creek War, Menawa led a party that assassinated Creek leader William McIntosh after he signed a treaty surrendering the last of the tribe's lands in Georgia. He was removed to Indian Territory with his fellow tribesmen in the 1830s.

STEPHEN MINOR

Stephen Minor was serving as acting governor of the Natchez District at the time of its transfer to American authorities in 1798. A Pennsylvania native, Minor had moved to the colony of Louisiana in the 1770s and served in various capacities with the Spanish government for nearly two decades at the time of the creation of the Mississippi Territory. The land grants he received as reward for his service enabled him to become one of the wealthiest men in the area. Minor worked with Andrew Ellicott to survey the boundary between the territory and Spanish West Florida.

Afterward, he lived as a planter in the Natchez area and served as president of the Bank of Mississippi. He died in 1815 and was buried in Natchez City Cemetery.

James Monroe

The fifth president of the United States (1817–1825), James Monroe, signed the 1817 legislation that created the state of Mississippi and the Alabama Territory, and in 1819, he signed the act admitting the state of Alabama to the union. He is the only sitting president to have visited Mississippi or Alabama prior to statehood, arriving in Huntsville in June 1819 during a tour of the South. Monroe Counties in Mississippi and Alabama, as well as the city of Monroeville, Alabama, are named in his honor.

Benajah Osmun

Benajah Osmun served as the commander of the Adams County militia from shortly after the formation of the Mississippi Territory until his resignation in 1806. A Revolutionary War veteran with a distinguished record of service, which included his participation in fighting at Quebec, Long Island and Charleston and twice being captured, he ended the war with the rank of lieutenant. He became an original member of the Society of Cincinnati, a patriotic hereditary organization founded after the war that is continued by descendants of officers in the Continental army. Osmun, a New Jersey native, moved to the Natchez area in 1790 and operated a plantation. He was an acquaintance of Aaron Burr and served as one of his bondsmen after his arrest in Natchez in 1807. Osmun died in 1815 and was buried on the grounds of his home, Windy Hill Manor.

Timothy Pickering

Timothy Pickering served as the United States secretary of state under Presidents George Washington and John Adams. The Massachusetts native and Revolutionary War veteran also served as the nation's postmaster general and as a congressman. A prominent leader in the Federalist Party at the time of the Mississippi Territory's organization, Pickering had the honor of having one of the state's first counties named for him. After the election of Democratic-Republican Thomas Jefferson, local officials at odds with the Federalists renamed the county in honor of Jefferson.

JOHN PITCHLYNN

John Pitchlynn worked among Mississippi's Choctaws for over forty years as a trader, interpreter and advisor. Owing to his self-taught fluency in the Choctaw language and his familiarity with tribal leaders, he played an influential role in negotiating several landmark treaties between the tribe and the federal government. During the Creek War, he helped persuade the Choctaw to fight against the Red Stick Creeks as an ally of the United States. Born in South Carolina, Pitchlynn moved to Choctaw country with his father as a young man in the 1770s. His two marriages to women of mixed Choctaw ancestry provided him unusual access to tribal affairs. One of his children, Peter, eventually became a prominent Choctaw leader in the 1830s. Pitchlynn died in 1835 as one of the wealthiest men in the Choctaw Nation.

GEORGE POINDEXTER

George Poindexter was one of the leading political figures in early Mississippi history. During his long and distinguished career, he served as a delegate to the territorial assembly, attorney general of the Mississippi Territory, a territorial judge and a territorial representative to the U.S. Congress. After Mississippi's statehood, he served as governor and as both a U.S. congressman and senator. Poindexter, who moved to the Mississippi Territory from his native Virginia, is credited with writing a large portion of Mississippi's first constitution.

LeRoy Pope

LeRoy Pope, sometimes referred to as the "father of Huntsville," was, for several decades, one of the most influential political leaders in the Tennessee Valley region. He moved to the area from Georgia about 1809 and soon became a wealthy planter. Through his strong connections with other recently arrived but prominent citizens from Georgia, he was able to become instrumental in the region's development during the territorial years and well into Alabama's early statehood era. Largely through his influence, the city of Huntsville was incorporated in 1811 under the name of Twickenham in honor of the home of English poet Alexander Pope. It was soon renamed in honor of pioneer settler John Hunt. Pope is buried in Huntsville's historic Maple Hill Cemetery.

Pushmataha

One of the most influential Native leaders of the early 1800s, Choctaw Chief Pushmataha was born circa 1764. In 1805, he became chief of the Six Towns Division of the Choctaws, one of the three principal political districts of the tribe. He served as an ally of United States forces during the Creek War and in the War of 1812, where he participated in the Battle of New Orleans. Pushmataha became a key negotiator in talks leading to removal of Native Americans from their ancestral lands in the years after Mississippi's statehood. In 1824, he died in Washington, D.C., where he had gone to seek resolution for illegal settlement on land promised his tribespeople in the West. He was buried in the Congressional Cemetery in Washington, D.C.

Pushmataha. *Courtesy of the Mississippi Department of Archives and History.*

112

THOMAS RODNEY

The namesake of the famous Mississippi ghost town of Rodney, Delaware native Thomas Rodney served as a judge in the Mississippi Territory from 1803 to 1811. He also held the position of land commissioner. Before moving to the Southwest, Rodney served in the Continental Congress, fought in the Revolutionary War and served in the Delaware state legislature. His brother, Caesar Rodney, was a signer of the Declaration of Independence. Ironically, Rodney may be most well-known today for his colorful chronicle of his grueling journey from Delaware to assume his post in the Mississippi Territory in 1803, edited and published in the 1990s as *A Journal Through the West*. Rodney died in Natchez in 1811.

WINTHROP SARGENT

A strict Puritan from Massachusetts, Winthrop Sargent served as the first governor of the Mississippi Territory. His autocratic style clashed immediately with the freedom-loving frontiersmen of the region. Many viewed his attempts to bring law and order to the territory, especially his series of laws derisively known as "Sargent's Codes," as usurpations of power. These opponents sent their grievances to the national government, which granted the territory the second stage of government that allowed for popular election for a legislative assembly. When Thomas Jefferson became president, he dismissed Sargent from office. He retired from public life and became a planter until his death in 1820. His grave is located in the Sargent family center near his plantation home, Gloucester, in Natchez.

WILLIAM B. SHIELDS

Maryland native William B. Shields held several positions in the territorial and early state governments of Mississippi. He served as a land claims agent, legislator and attorney general in the Mississippi Territory and as one of the first judges of the state supreme court as well as a judge on the United States District Court for the District of Mississippi. A lawyer who moved to the territory in 1803, Shields had previously served as the secretary of state of Delaware. He died in Natchez in 1823.

Fulwar Skipwith

Fulwar Skipwith served as governor of the short-lived Republic of West Florida in 1810. A Virginia native, he served in the American Revolution and as consul to West Indian island nations and France prior to settling on a plantation near Baton Rouge in 1809. Skipwith took a leading role in the rebellion against Spanish authority in the region in 1810 and attempted to run it as a separate state before accepting annexation by the United States. Skipwith resided in Baton Rouge for the rest of his life as a prominent member of the community. He died in 1839.

Tecumseh

Born in what is now Ohio, Tecumseh became a leading figure in resistance to American settlement of Native lands in the early nineteenth century. He is most remembered for promoting the concept of a united Indian Confederacy along with his brother, the prophet Tenskwatawa. Tecumseh traveled to the Southeast from his native Great Lakes region in 1811 to rally regional tribes to his cause, addressing the gathered Creeks at their annual council meeting at Tuckabatchee. His appearance is credited with helping spark the Red Stick movement among a disgruntled nativist faction of the tribe. He fought as an ally of the British during the War of 1812 in several actions in the Detroit River region. He was killed in the Battle of the Thames on October 5, 1813.

Harry Toulmin

One of the most influential officials in the eastern section of the Mississippi Territory, Harry Toulmin served as a judge from 1804 to 1817. He also served in the same capacity in the Alabama Territory from its creation in 1817 to statehood in 1819. Toulmin was born in England and trained as a minister before moving to America and settling in Kentucky. There, he served as president of Transylvania Seminary and as Kentucky's secretary of state, and he took up the study of law prior to his appointment as a judge in the Mississippi Territory. From his office at Fort Stoddert, Toulmin helped create and enforce laws in the region for the remainder of the territorial period. Toulmin served in Alabama's Constitutional Convention in 1819, and in 1823, he compiled the Digest of the Laws of the State of Alabama, which included statutes of the Mississippi and Alabama Territories. He died on December 11, 1823, in Washington County, Alabama. A plaque honoring him stands at the Baldwin County courthouse in Bay Minette, Alabama.

WILLIAM WEATHERFORD ("RED EAGLE")

William Weatherford. *From Red Eagle and the Wars with the Creek Indians of Alabama, by George Cary Eggleston.* James Wilkinson. *Courtesy of Independence National Historical Park.*

The son of a Creek woman and a Scottish trader, William Weatherford sided with the Red Sticks in the Creek War. He helped plan the attacks on Fort Mims and at Calabee Creek and is often remembered for his daring escape from the Battle of the Holy Ground, in which he leaped his horse into the Alabama River. Weatherford voluntarily surrendered to Andrew Jackson at the end of the Creek War and used his influence to persuade other Red Sticks to lay down their arms. He lived as a planter in Alabama until his death in 1824. He is buried in William Weatherford Memorial Park in Baldwin County, Alabama, where monuments mark his grave and that of his mother, Sehoy Tate Weatherford.

CATO WEST

Cato West was an instrumental political figure during Mississippi's territorial period. A member of the prominent Green-West Republican faction, West opposed the Federalist administration of Winthrop Sargent. Ambitious to a fault, while serving as secretary for the territory, West hoped to be selected as the new governor after W.C.C. Claiborne left office. When he was not chosen,

West returned to his estate and took the government records with him, only returning them after threats from the legislature. Later, as a delegate to the constitutional convention in 1817, he refused to sign the document due to his unhappiness with the border location between Mississippi and Alabama.

GENERAL JAMES WILKINSON

A career military officer, James Wilkinson was involved in a number of major events in the Southeast. A veteran of the Revolutionary War, he, along with W.C.C. Claiborne, accepted the transfer of Louisiana from the French after the Louisiana Purchase was signed. As head of the Seventh Military District, Wilkinson led the American force that seized Fort Charlotte and the disputed territory of West Florida from Spain in April 1813. Later in the War of 1812, he led two unsuccessful campaigns against the British on the Canadian border. He was widely unpopular, a poor administrator and secretly worked as a spy for Spain for many years.

ROBERT WILLIAMS

Robert Williams was a land commissioner for the Mississippi Territory before he became governor in 1805. A native of North Carolina, Williams's irascible temperament was ill suited to rule a territory racked by political factionalism. He bickered constantly with those around him, typified by his feud with territory secretary Cowles Mead during the Aaron Burr conspiracy. He even dissolved the territorial assembly on several occasions. His growing unpopularity, fueled by land claim disputes and citizens' displeasure at his frequent absences to his home state, led to his resignation in 1809.

HISTORIC SITES

Alabama (North)

ALABAMA CONSTITUTION VILLAGE
109 Gates Avenue Southeast
Huntsville, Alabama
www.earlyworks.com/Alabama-constitution-village

A living history museum interpreting life in early nineteenth-century Alabama, Constitution Village features several reconstructed historic buildings available for tour, including a law office, print shop, land surveyor's office and post office. A reconstruction of the cabinet shop where Alabama's 1819 constitutional convention met stands at the corner of Gates and Franklin Streets.

BATTLE OF TALLADEGA MEMORIAL
Corner of West Battle Street and South Spring Street
Talladega, Alabama

Talladega was the site of an allied Creek village that came under siege by Red Stick Creeks in the fall of 1813. Andrew Jackson led his troops there in assistance of the besieged allies, fighting and winning the Battle of Talladega on November 9, 1813. Another monument to those who fought in the battle stands in the nearby city cemetery, and a historic marker for the event stands on the grounds of the county courthouse downtown.

BIG SPRING PARK
200 Church Street Northwest
Huntsville, Alabama

Big Spring Park is the site of the natural limestone spring around which the community of Huntsville developed in the early 1800s. John Hunt, credited with founding the town, built his cabin on the bluff above the spring circa 1805.

EDDINS HOUSE
BURRITT ON THE MOUNTAIN
3101 Burritt Drive
Huntsville, Alabama
www.burrittonthemountain.com

Built in 1808, the Eddins House is believed to be the oldest dwelling of any kind in the state of Alabama. The home originally stood near the community of Ardmore, north of Huntsville, but is now part of the collection of historic structures at Burritt on the Mountain, an educational park on Monte Sano Mountain.

FORT STROTHER MONUMENT
Intersection of Highway 144 and Valley Drive
Ohatchee, Alabama

Fort Strother served as the primary advance supply base during Andrew Jackson's campaigns against the Red Sticks. Named after John Strother, Jackson's topographical engineer, the fort was built in November 1813 on the Coosa River at a spot known as Ten Islands. From this fort, Jackson moved to relieve the friendly Creeks besieged at Talladega and, later on, launched a foray that resulted in the battles of Emuckfau and Enitichapoco Creeks. Fort Strother was also the location where Jackson was forced to deal with the near mutiny of his troops. A historic marker and interpretive signage for Fort Strother is located in St. Clair County on Highway 144 near the Henry-Neely Dam on the Coosa River.

Battle of Talladega Memorial. *Photograph by Mike Bunn*.

Eddins House at Burritt on the Mountain in Huntsville, Alabama. *Photograph by Mike Bunn*.

HICKMAN LOG CABIN
POND SPRING
12280 Highway 20
Hillsboro, Alabama
www.ahc.alabama.gov

A dogtrot cabin built in 1818, this building is located at Pond Spring, the plantation home of General Joe Wheeler. It was built by the original owners of the property, the John P. Hickman family. The site is operated as a house museum by the Alabama Historical Commission.

INITIAL SURVEY POINT HISTORIC MARKER
Highway 231/431
Just South of the Tennessee State Line, North of Huntsville, Alabama

Surveyor Thomas Freeman, in 1809, established a marker at this spot, which was used as the baseline for all subsequent property surveys in northern Alabama. It has become known as the Huntsville Meridian.

JOHN LOONEY HOUSE
4187 Greensport Road
Ashville, Alabama

Built between 1818 and 1820 by Creek War veteran and Tennessee native John Looney and his family, the Looney House is the oldest two-story dogtrot home in Alabama. One of the best examples of pioneer architecture in Alabama, it is operated as a historic house museum by the St. Clair County Historical Society. Tours are available by appointment: 205-629-6897.

HISTORIC MOORESVILLE
www.mooresvilleal.com

Incorporated in 1818 by the Alabama territorial legislature, Mooresville is one of Alabama's most historic communities. The entire town is listed in the National Register of Historic Places. The small town contains several homes that date to the early statehood era and other structures, such as churches and its circa 1840 post office, which date to later in the antebellum period.

Stagecoach Inn and Tavern at Mooresville, Alabama. *Photograph by Clay Williams.*

OVERTON FARM

Overton Farm Road
Off Highway 172, North of Hodges, Alabama

About 1819, early area settler Abner Overton built a log cabin on this spot, to which he gradually added rooms over the years as he operated a farm along Bear Creek. Only the double pen dogtrot cabin at the complex's core remains. For access, call Rock Creek Canyon Equestrian Park: 205-935-3499.

POPE MANSION

403 Echols Avenue
Huntsville, Alabama
Private Residence

The oldest original building in the city of Huntsville and possibly the oldest brick building in the state of Alabama, the Pope Mansion was constructed in 1814 by influential political figure LeRoy Pope.

SADLER PLANTATION HOUSE
Eastern Valley Road, Approximately One Mile South of I-459
McCalla, Alabama

The core of this historic home is a single pen log cabin that was constructed in 1817 by early settler John Loveless. According to oral tradition, Loveless built his cabin in an old Native field shortly after arriving in the area from South Carolina. Later owners, the Sadler family, enclosed the structure with additions. Tours may be arranged through the West Jefferson County Historical Society: 205-426-1633.

THE PUBLIC INN
205 Williams Avenue Southeast
Huntsville, Alabama
Private Residence

This rare Federal-period structure dates to 1818. An inn in which some delegates to the 1819 constitutional convention are believed to have boarded, the building originally stood a few blocks away and was moved to its current location in the 1920s.

WEEDEN HOUSE
300 Gates Avenue
Huntsville, Alabama
www.weedenhousemuseum.com

Constructed in 1819 by Henry C. Bradford, the Weeden House is most closely associated with the family of Dr. William Weeden, who purchased the property in 1845. Today, the home is a museum operated by the city of Huntsville, interpreting local history.

ALABAMA (CENTRAL)

FORT MITCHELL HISTORIC SITE AND THE CHATTAHOOCHEE INDIAN HERITAGE CENTER
561 Alabama Highway 165
Fort Mitchell, Alabama
www.alabama/travel/places-to-go/russell-county-historical-commission-historic-fort-mitchell

The site features a reconstruction of the 1813 fort that stood nearby and from which General John Floyd launched two major offensives into Red Stick territory, an early settler cabin that was moved to the grounds, a historic cemetery and a museum and visitor's center. Adjacent to the park is the Chattahoochee Indian Heritage Center, an outdoor museum commemorating the Chattahoochee Valley's rich Native heritage and the saga of Native removal.

FORT TOULOUSE–FORT JACKSON PARK
2521 West Fort Toulouse Road
Wetumpka, Alabama

Fort Toulouse–Fort Jackson Park contains a replica of an eighteenth-century French fort, as well as a partial reconstruction of Fort Jackson, where the treaty ending the Creek War was signed. The site also contains reproduction Creek houses, a visitor center and museum and a nature trail. After the American victory at Horseshoe Bend, Andrew Jackson led his men south toward the Hickory Ground at the confluence of the Coosa and Tallapoosa Rivers, believed to be the last major gathering spot for hostile Red Sticks. Finding no resistance, Jackson's troops helped construct Fort Jackson on the site where the French had built Fort Toulouse in 1717. Fort Jackson became a gathering place for surrendering Red Sticks as well as friendly Creeks in search of food. The epic meeting of Jackson and William Weatherford took place here.

HOLY GROUND BATTLEFIELD PARK
300 Battlefield Road
Lowndesboro, Alabama

This recreational park along the Alabama River, maintained by the U.S. Army Corps of Engineers, is located on the site of a fortified Red Stick town that was attacked and destroyed by troops under the command of General Ferdinand L. Claiborne in December 1813. It was here that William Weatherford, astride his horse Arrow, made his famous escape by leaping his horse into the Alabama River. The park contains a historic marker and interpretive signage commemorating the battle.

HORSESHOE BEND NATIONAL MILITARY PARK
11288 Horseshoe Bend Road
Daviston, Alabama
www.nps.gov/hobe

This tranquil historic park, located in a horseshoe-shaped bend in the Tallapoosa River, witnessed one of the most vicious battles ever fought on Alabama soil. On March 27, 1814, the culminating battle of Andrew Jackson's campaign against the Red Sticks raged on these grounds and effectively ended the Creek War. Whereas Jackson's army suffered fewer than two hundred casualties, nearly nine hundred Red Sticks lost their lives. More Natives were killed here that day than in any other battle in United States history. The park features driving and hiking tours of the battlefield and a visitor's center/museum.

LUCAS TAVERN
IN OLD ALABAMA TOWN
301 North Hull Street
Montgomery, Alabama

Built around 1818, the tavern is the oldest structure in Montgomery County. It was moved here from its original location along the Federal Road east of town in the 1970s. A rare surviving example of a roadside tavern of the era, it hosted Lafayette during his visit to Alabama in 1825.

MUSEUM OF ALABAMA
624 Washington Avenue
Montgomery, Alabama
www.archives.alabama.gov

Located inside the home of the Alabama Department of Archives and History, this museum contains exhibits chronicling the entire history of Alabama. These exhibits contain hundreds of artifacts, images and documents that tell the story of struggles over the land, the rise of a cotton economy, the Civil War, industrialization, world wars, civil rights, the race to the moon and more. Exhibits on the territorial period detail the story of the Creek War and the process toward Alabama's statehood.

OLD CAHAWBA ARCHAEOLOGICAL PARK
9518 Cahaba Road
Orrville, Alabama
www.ahc.alabama.gov

The park preserves the site of the ghost town of Cahawba, the location of Alabama's first state capital. The town was laid out in 1819 and rose to become one of the state's leading trading centers before languishing in the latter half of the nineteenth century. The park features a visitor's center, an organized driving or hiking tour, ruins of several historic structures associated with the antebellum town, a small number of intact structures dating to the era of Cahawba's heyday, cemeteries and scenic views of the confluence of the Cahaba and Alabama Rivers. The park also includes the site of a Civil War prison and the remnants of an earthen moat built by Natives who occupied a fortified village on the site over five hundred years ago.

SITE OF TUCKAUBATCHEE
Highway 229
Just Outside of Tallassee, Alabama
Private Property

Tuckaubatchee was a major Creek population and political center located on the west bank of the Tallapoosa River, just south of the modern city of Tallassee. The town hosted the Creeks' annual council and is where Tecumseh made his impassioned speech in September 1811, urging them to recover their ancestral ways. A historic marker stands near the site of the town on the west side of Highway 229, approximately five miles north of I-85. An older stone monument commemorating the town stands in front of city hall on Freeman Avenue in Tallassee.

VINE AND OLIVE COMPANY HISTORICAL MARKER

Demopolis, Alabama, traces its history to the French exiles of the Vine and Olive Company, who settled in the area at the invitation of the United States government during the territorial period. Although their experiment in growing grapes and olives as cash crops was a failure and most of the immigrants remained here only a short time, the colony and communities they established (Aigleville and Demopolis) are remembered as an important part of Alabama's territorial years. A historic marker commemorating the community stands on Highway 80 at the eastern city limits of Demopolis.

ALABAMA (SOUTH)

ELLICOTT STONE
Highway 43 North
In the Vicinity of the Community of Bucks, Alabama, Between Mile Markers 18 And 19

This stone marker was placed April 10, 1799, by a crew led by Andrew Ellicott during the survey that delineated the boundary between the Mississippi Territory and the Spanish colony of West Florida. The line Ellicott established remained the border between the United States and Spain in the region until its annexation by the United States during the War of 1812.

FORT BOWYER SITE
FORT MORGAN STATE HISTORIC SITE
Highway 180
Gulf Shores, Alabama
www.ahc.alabama.gov

Fort Bowyer, a War of 1812 fortification defending Mobile, stood on the site of Fort Morgan a generation prior to the famous Civil War Battle of Mobile Bay. It came under British assault twice during the conflict, in September 1814 and February 1815. While the majority of interpretation at Fort Morgan National Historic Landmark focuses on the Civil War era, interpretive panels explain its predecessor's significance.

FORT CLAIBORNE SITE
Hwy. 84 at the Alabama River
Perdue Hill, AL

General Ferdinand L. Claiborne oversaw the construction of Fort Claiborne in November 1813. The fort, approximately 200 feet square and featuring three blockhouses and a battery of artillery, was located along the Alabama River on a 150-foot-high limestone outcropping known as "Weatherford's Bluff." From this location, Claiborne led a force of approximately one thousand men on a campaign against the Holy Ground in December 1813.

A stone monument commemorating the fort and the community of Claiborne that grew up around the fort stands on the north side of Highway 84 in Monroe County, Alabama, near the crossing of the Alabama River.

FORT CONDE RECONSTRUCTION
150 South Royal Street
Mobile, Alabama
www.historymuseumofmobile.com

Fort Conde is a scale reconstruction of the outpost originally built by the French founders of Mobile in the early 1700s and occupied for nearly a century after successively by the British, Spanish and American armies. This is the location where General James Wilkinson accepted the surrender of Spanish forces in April 1813, marking the beginning of official United States control of those portions of the Gulf Coast that were annexed into the Mississippi Territory. The fort is operated by the History Museum of Mobile.

FORT MIMS HISTORIC SITE
www.ahc.alabama.gov

Built around several structures on the plantation of prominent planter Samuel Mims, Fort Mims was the site of one of the most consequential calamities in American military history. On August 30, 1813, the fort was attacked and destroyed by a Red Stick force of about 700 warriors both as a preemptory strike and as retaliation for being ambushed at Burnt Corn Creek a month earlier. Nearly 250 of the settlers, allied Creeks and members of the Mississippi Territorial and local militias living in the one-acre facility at the time were killed in the day-long struggle. The news of the disaster jolted the nation and galvanized Americans, especially those living in states bordering the Mississippi Territory, in support of measures to put down the perceived rebellion. Fort Mims Park, operated by the Fort Mims Restoration Association, is located at the original fort site (owned by the Alabama Historical Commission), just off County Road 80 in northwestern Baldwin County. The park features a partial

Reconstruction of Fort Mims. *Photograph by Mike Bunn.*

reconstruction of the fort, detailed interpretive signage explaining the battle and a small museum.

FORT SINQUEFIELD HISTORICAL PARK
Fort Sinquefield Road, Off Highway 84
Whatley, Alabama

Interpreting the Creek War Battle of Fort Sinquefield, this small park stands on the site of a settler fort that came under attack by Red Sticks on September 2, 1813. It features several interpretive panels around the perimeter of the fort, a partial reconstruction of one of its walls and a walking trail. A short distance away on the north side of Highway 84 stands a historic marker commemorating the Kimbell-James Massacre, an event that is closely related to the attack on Fort Sinquefield.

FORT STODDERT SITE AND MOUNT VERNON CANTONMENT
County Road 96
Mount Vernon, Alabama

Built in 1799, Fort Stoddert served as a port of entry to the United States until the annexation of the Spanish colony of West Florida into the Mississippi Territory. The actual site of the fort on the Mobile River (approximately three miles east of Highway 43) is unmarked, but its history is interpreted in the form of a history trail and historic markers relating the fort's history and that of closely related Mount Vernon Cantonment nearby. There is also a memorial to Mississippi Territory Judge Ephraim Kirby. A mile west along County Road 96 stand the Mount Vernon Arsenal and Barracks, the site of the Mount Vernon Cantonment.

HISTORIC BLAKELEY STATE PARK
34745 Highway 225
Spanish Fort, Alabama
www.blakeleypark.com

Site of one of early Alabama's largest cities, Blakeley is a 2,100-acre historical park located along the Tensaw River that preserves Native, colonial era and early American cultural heritage features. The park is most famous for being the site of the state's largest Civil War battlefield (the Battle of Fort Blakeley). The park also offers camping, cabins and dozens of miles of hiking, biking and horseback riding trails in addition to a year-round schedule of guided cruises into the Mobile-Tensaw Delta.

HISTORY MUSEUM OF MOBILE
111 South Royal Street
Mobile, Alabama
www.historymuseumofmobile.com

Containing over twenty thousand square feet of exhibit space, the museum interprets Mobile's history from pre-colonial contact to the modern Port City. Exhibits on the colonial and territorial eras detail Mobile's role in these pivotal eras of regional history.

OLD ST. STEPHENS HISTORICAL PARK
Off County Road 34
St. Stephens, Alabama
www.oldststephens.net

Site of the capital of the Alabama Territory, St. Stephens hosted its two legislative sessions. Founded by the Spanish in the 1790s as a military outpost and incorporated as an American town in 1811, it was once one of Alabama's largest cities. Today, visitors can walk the original streets of St. Stephens and discover where landmarks such as the Globe Hotel once stood.

THE FEDERAL ROAD

A postal route cleared in the first decade of the 1800s connecting central Georgia with what is now Southwest Alabama, the Federal Road served as a primary immigration route for American settlers during the territorial and early statehood periods. The original route of the road, which roughly parallels Highway 80, running between Phenix City and Montgomery, and I-65 between Montgomery and Mobile, can be traced for short distances in several areas of east and south Alabama. Several modern roadways follow sections of the road. One of the longest and easiest-to-follow sections of the original road (nearly thirty miles long) can be found along the Conecuh-Monroe County, Alabama border. Conecuh County Road 5 from Skinnerton to its intersection with Highway 84 follows closely the original route of the Federal Road for over twenty miles. Several historic markers are located along the road's route in Alabama.

MISSISSIPPI (NORTH)

THE CEDARS
1305 Military Road
Columbus, Mississippi
Private Residence

Believed to be the oldest surviving house in north Mississippi, The Cedars began as a one-room log cabin around 1818. Captain Edward Randolph, a veteran of the War of 1812, later enlarged the structure.

COTTON GIN PORT SITE
Intersection of U.S. 278 and Cotton Gin Road
Amory, Mississippi

Named for a cotton gin built here by the federal government for the Chickasaw, the community of Cotton Gin Port was an important trade and population center during Mississippi's territorial and early statehood years. The community was located at the southern terminus of Gaines Trace, near the head of navigation of the Tombigbee River. It survived until the 1880s, when the railroad running through the area bypassed it, and much of its surviving population and businesses relocated to nearby Amory.

GAINES TRACE HISTORICAL MARKER
Highway 25, Just East of Intersection with Smithville Road
Smithville, Mississippi

This road, connecting the Tennessee and Tombigbee Rivers, was surveyed by its namesake, Edmund P. Gaines, prior to 1810.

NATCHEZ TRACE PARKWAY VISITOR'S CENTER
2680 Natchez Trace Parkway (Milepost 266)
Tupelo, Mississippi
www.nps.gov/natr

The Parkway Visitor's Center serves as the headquarters of the parkway that is a 444-mile journey through history, connecting Nashville, Tennessee and Natchez, Mississippi. It contains exhibits on the trace's history and an introductory film.

MISSISSIPPI (CENTRAL)

COWLES MEAD CEMETERY
Milepost 88.1 on Natchez Trace
Clinton, Mississippi

Cowles Mead held several political offices during the territorial period, including territorial secretary and territorial governor. While serving as governor, he ordered the arrest of Aaron Burr. He eventually moved to the Jackson area, where he built his home, Greenwood, which burned in 1863. Nothing remains of the estate but the family cemetery.

DOAK'S STAND
Interpretive Signage Stands at Milepost 128.4 on the Natchez Trace

The Treaty of Doak's Stand was signed in October 1820 at a tavern on the Natchez Trace in current-day Madison County, Mississippi. The Choctaw Nation ceded more than five million acres, dramatically altering Mississippi's trajectory and prompting the removal of the capital away from the river counties to the central part of the state. The future capital (Jackson) and the county in which it is located (Hinds) were named after treaty commissioners Andrew Jackson and Thomas Hinds.

LEFLEUR'S BLUFF STATE PARK
3315 Lakeland Terrace
Jackson, Mississippi

Rising twenty feet above the Pearl River in Jackson, LeFleur's Bluff was selected as the capital of Mississippi. Named after French trader Louis Le Fleur, the site met the requirements for an appropriate site, such as high ground, good water, healthful air and fertile soil. No historic marker exists, but the park features hiking trails that run along the Pearl River.

TWO MISSISSIPPI MUSEUMS
222 North Street
Jackson, Mississippi
www.2mm.mdah.ms.gov

Operated by the Mississippi Department of Archives and History, the Mississippi Civil Rights Museum and the Museum of Mississippi History tell the dramatic history of Mississippi. The Museum of Mississippi History contains exhibits on Mississippi's territorial and early statehood periods.

MISSISSIPPI (SOUTH)

AUBURN
400 Duncan Avenue
Natchez, Mississippi

Built in 1812 for the Mississippi Territory's Attorney General Lyman Harding, Auburn is a National Historic Landmark. The home is credited with being the first in Natchez to follow an established architectural plan, and it influenced the design of numerous homes across the South. Noted doctor and civic leader Stephen Duncan bought the home after Harding's death. His family owned the home until the early 1900s, when it was donated to the city. Regular tours are offered; for a schedule visit www.auburnmuseum.org.

ELIZABETH FEMALE ACADEMY
Ruins and Signage Located at Milepost 5.1 on the Natchez Trace

Operating between 1818 and 1845, the Elizabeth Female Academy was the first female institution of higher learning charted by Mississippi and the first institution to offer degrees to women in the state. It was named after Elizabeth Roach, who donated the land.

JOHN FORD HOME
142 John Ford Home Road
Sandy Hook, Mississippi

Built around 1800 by frontier minister John Ford, this home was the site of the famous Pearl River Convention of October 1816. The assembly gathered to discuss whether the Mississippi Territory should move toward statehood as one or two states and resulted in the selection of a delegate, Judge Harry Toulmin, who was sent to the nation's capital to lobby for its position. The home is owned and managed by the Marion County Historical Society and is open for tours by appointment: 601-731-3999.

FORKS OF THE ROAD SLAVE MARKET
Intersection of D'Evereaux Drive, Liberty Road and St. Catherine Street
Natchez, Mississippi

This outdoor park, located on the site of one of the South's largest slave markets, interprets its history and the larger story of the slave trade in the region.

FORT ADAMS
Historic Marker located on Main Street
Woodville, Mississippi

Constructed in 1799, Fort Adams was built after the Spanish abandoned the Natchez District. It served as a U.S. port of entry on the Mississippi River before the acquisition of New Orleans. A treaty with the Choctaws was signed there in 1801. No visible evidence of the fort remains today. The community of Fort Adams lies near the location of the fort.

Site of the Forks of the Road Slave Market in Natchez. *Courtesy of Lance Harris.*

FORT ROSALIE
528 South Canal Street
Natchez, Mississippi

Originally built by the French in 1716, this fort sat atop the bluff at Natchez and guarded the river. Later renamed Fort Panmure by the British, the fort was maintained by the Spanish at the time of its transfer to the United States. Today, there is a green space maintained by the National Park Service, with picnic tables and interpretive signage. The site is open from sunrise to sunset.

GLOUCESTER
201 Lower Woodville Road
Natchez, Mississippi
Private Residence

One of the best examples of Federal-style architecture in Mississippi, Gloucester was built about 1803. In 1807, it became the home of Winthrop Sargent, first governor of the Mississippi Territory.

GOVERNOR HOLMES HOUSE
207 South Wall Street
Natchez, Mississippi
Private Residence

David Holmes, the last governor of the Mississippi Territory and the first governor of the state of Mississippi, lived here after purchasing the home in 1821. The home was built in 1794 and is one of the few surviving structures from Natchez's colonial days.

HISTORIC JEFFERSON COLLEGE
16 Old North Street
Natchez, Mississippi
www.mdah.state.ms.us

The first institution of higher learning chartered in the Mississippi Territory (1802), Jefferson College opened in 1811 and operated through the Civil War. When it reopened, it did so as a preparatory school. It continued in this capacity until its final closure in 1964. Its oldest surviving building is the East Wing, constructed in 1819. The historic site is currently closed; the Mississippi Department of Archives and History has plans to open a Natchez Center for American History there in the future.

Mississippi Constitutional Convention Monument in Washington, Mississippi.
Photograph by Clay Williams.

Near the entrance to the historic site is a monument commemorating the Mississippi Constitutional Convention of 1817. The convention met a few hundred yards away at a Methodist church that no longer stands, and the state's first legislature convened nearby at DeFrance's Tavern, also known as Assembly Hall. That structure was destroyed in a fire in the 1990s, but the ruins of its foundation can still be seen near the intersection of Highway 61 and Assembly Street. A historic marker is located by the ruins. The site is owned by the Mississippi Department of Archives and History.

HOUSE ON ELLICOTT HILL
211 North Canal Street
Natchez, Mississippi
www.visitnatchez.org

The construction on this house, which stands on the hill overlooking the Mississippi River, began in 1798. It was made forever famous by being the location of Andrew Ellicott's raising of the American flag in defiance of Spanish attempts to delay their withdrawal from the region following their cession of the area in the Treaty of San Lorenzo. Tours are offered; for a schedule, check with the Natchez Visitor's Center.

LA POINTE–KREBS HOUSE, "OLD SPANISH FORT"
4602 Fort Street
Pascagoula, Mississippi
www.lapointkrebs.org

Built in 1757, the La Pointe–Krebs House is the oldest structure in Mississippi and the oldest confirmed building in the entire Mississippi Valley. The Krebs family lived here during the territorial period. Near the house is a historic marker commemorating the early experiment in producing a cotton gin by the Krebs family, which predated Eli Whitney's by over a decade.

LINDEN
1 Connor Circle
Natchez, Mississippi
www.lindenbandb.com

This mansion is among the oldest homes in Natchez; its central portion dates to the late 1700s, while the east wing was constructed in 1818. While the home was originally known as Oaklands, United States Senator and Mississippi Attorney General Thomas Buck Reed renamed it Reedland during his ownership of the property. Its next owner, Dr. John Ker, gave it its current name. The home is currently a bed-and-breakfast.

MISSISSIPPI BAPTIST BEGINNINGS EXHIBIT
Highway 61 Between Fayette and Natchez

This outdoor exhibit of a series of interpretive panels placed by the Mississippi Baptist Historical Commission provides details on the development of the Baptist Church in Mississippi's territorial and early statehood period. It is located near the site of the first Baptist church founded in the area in 1791, during the years of Spanish administration of the region.

MONMOUTH
1358 John A. Quitman Boulevard
Natchez, Mississippi
www.monmouthhistoricinn.com

Monmouth is a National Historic Landmark built in 1818 by Natchez postmaster John Hankinson. The home is most closely associated with noted Mississippi political leader John A. Quitman, who bought the home in 1824 and lived there the remainder of his life. It is currently a bed-and-breakfast.

MOUNT LOCUST
Located at Milepost 15.5 of the Natchez Trace
www.nps.gov/places/mount-locust-historic-home.htm

Constructed circa 1780, Mount Locust served as both a working plantation and an inn, where weary travelers could rest as they traveled along the Natchez

Trace. Mount Locust is the only surviving stand (or inn) of the fifty or so that were once in existence along the Trace.

NATCHEZ UNDER THE HILL
Silver Street
Natchez, Mississippi

The area known as Natchez Under-the-Hill was one of the rowdiest ports on the Mississippi River. This location witnessed keelboats, flatboats and eventually steamboats dock to unload their precious cargo of commodities. This underside of the more proper Natchez, located on the bluff above, featured taverns, gambling halls and brothels lining the street awaiting their opportunity to separate the travelers from their hard-earned money.

OLD GREENVILLE
Highway 553 at Mable Aldridge Road
About 6 Miles West of Highway 61, Near Fayette

The original seat of Jefferson County, Mississippi, Greenville was an important commercial center in the state's territorial years. The town, which began as a small settlement around the home of early settler Henry Green, was officially incorporated in 1805. The town stood approximately midway between Natchez and Port Gibson. With the removal of the county seat in 1825, Greenville quickly declined and is today a ghost town.

ST. STEPHENS ROAD HISTORIC MARKER
Intersection of U.S. 51 and Dale Trail Northeast
Brookhaven, Mississippi

The St. Stephens Road, opened in 1811, was the main wagon road connecting Natchez with St. Stephens. Another older historic marker commemorating the route stands at the intersection of County Roads 184 and 43 in Monticello, Mississippi.

Texada in Natchez,
Mississippi.
*Photograph by Clay
Williams.*

TEXADA
222 South Wall Street
Natchez, Mississippi
Private Residence

The construction of Texada began circa 1793. The structure is believed to be the oldest brick building in Natchez. The house served as the capitol for the state of Mississippi from 1818 to 1820.

WINCHESTER SITE
U.S. Highway 45 at Winchester Cross Road
Waynesboro, Mississippi

The site of the town of Winchester is commemorated by a historic marker just south of the modern city of Waynesboro. The site of a Creek War fortification (Patton's Fort) and located near the Chickasaway River and a major road connecting Natchez and the state of Georgia, the community was chartered in 1818. It served as the seat of Wayne County until after the Civil War. Nothing remains of the community today.

MAPS OF THE MISSISSIPPI TERRITORY AND THE NEW STATES OF MISSISSIPPI AND ALABAMA

The maps shown here represent the bulk of those of the Mississippi Territory and the new states of Mississippi and Alabama that were published during the era. They demonstrate the slow but steady development of the region, revealing its gradual transition from Native domain to American states and showcasing the pace and location of American settlement. They also show the persistent time lag in information about the territory in its actuality making its way to the publishing houses that produced American atlases of the time. It could frequently take over a decade for the locations of major communities to show up on widely available maps such as these. Much of the information about the region was simply reprinted from earlier maps, making many of those published prior to statehood, when more detailed information from land surveys became available, appear very similar. Taken together, they offer a unique visual depiction of an expansive and dynamic region during its formative years as it took shape over time.

THE MISSISSIPPI TERRITORY

Drawn by Samuel Lewis and Engraved by D. Fairman (1804)
Courtesy of the David Rumsey Map Collection

Published in 1804 in Samuel Lewis and Aaron Arrowsmith's *A New and Elegant General Atlas*, this map is the earliest known representation of the Mississippi

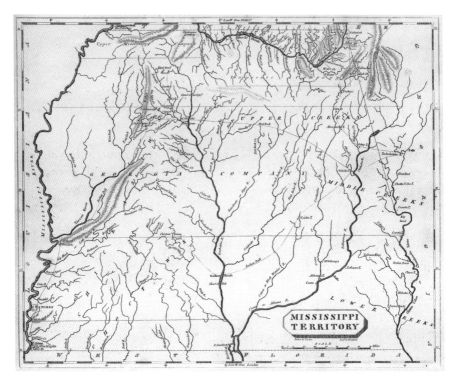

The Mississippi Territory, drawn by Samuel Lewis and engraved by D. Fairman, 1804. *Courtesy of the David Rumsey Map Collection.*

Territory as a distinct political entity. The map shows the territory prior to the acquisition of portions of the Spanish colony of West Florida along the Gulf Coast, but after the cession of claims by the state of Georgia to land between the Tennessee state line and the northern boundary of the original territory just north of the thirty-second parallel. There are a few trading posts, American fortifications and paths shown on the map, but only two American communities: the city of Natchez and the village of Clarksville to its south, along the West Florida border. The detailed labeling of every river and small stream throughout the territory shows it was not a totally unexplored province, but at the time of this map's creation, the Mississippi Territory was undeniably an expansive Native domain under only nominal control by the United States. Almost all communities indicated on the map are Native villages. The wide-ranging lands of the Creek, Choctaw and Chickasaw are noted, as are the controversial claims of the extralegal land companies (Georgia Company, Tennessee Company and Upper Mississippi Company), which sought to sell acreage in the area originally claimed by Georgia.

THE MISSISSIPPI TERRITORY AND GEORGIA

Published by Matthew Carey (1806)
Courtesy of the Normal B. Levanthal Map and Education Center at the Boston Public Library

Originally published in 1806 as part of noted Philadelphia publisher Matthew Carey's *American Minor Atlas*, this map is one of the few known works of cartography that depicted the Mississippi Territory prior to the annexation of portions of the Spanish colony of West Florida on the Gulf Coast. As is the case with the first known map of the territory published two years prior, this chart shows a region with few American communities; Natchez is the only American town of any size, though the village of Pinckneyville appears on the border with West Florida for the first time. Native villages dominate the map. The Natchez Trace and the new St. Stephens Road, connecting the Mississippi River settlements with the lower Alabama/Tombigbee River region, are featured prominently.

The Mississippi Territory and Georgia, published by Matthew Carey, 1806. *Courtesy of the Normal B. Levanthal Map and Education Center at the Boston Public Library.*

THE MISSISSIPPI TERRITORY

By Matthew Carey, Engraved by Francis Shallus (1814)
Courtesy of the David Rumsey Map Collection

This is among the first maps to depict the Mississippi Territory after the annexation of portions of West Florida. Aside from the revised borders showing the city of Mobile and the settlement at Biloxi being a part of the territory, very little has changed from the first map of it printed a decade earlier. A few new communities show up near Natchez, such as Ellicottville and Huntston. There is also a bit more detail on the location of important Native villages, especially those of the Creeks in the eastern section of the territory. This map appeared in Matthew Carey's *General Atlas*, published in 1814. The publication is recognized as the first atlas produced in the United States to feature standard color maps. Francis Shallus of Philadelphia engraved it.

THE MISSISSIPPI TERRITORY

By Matthew Carey and Benjamin Warner (1816)
Courtesy of the David Rumsey Map Collection

This map appeared in Cary and Warner's *A General Atlas*, one of several editions of the publication depicting the states of the United States and various countries across the globe. It is very similar to previous maps of the territory, with trading posts, Native villages and waterways being the most prominent features of the still sparsely settled region. While at least seven counties in what became Alabama and over a dozen in what became Mississippi had already been formed by this time, these units do not appear on maps until after Mississippi's statehood.

Opposite, top: The Mississippi Territory, by Matthew Carey, engraved by Francis Shallus, 1814. *Courtesy of the David Rumsey Map Collection.*

Opposite, bottom: The Mississippi Territory, by Matthew Carey and Benjamin Warner, 1816. *Courtesy of the David Rumsey Map Collection.*

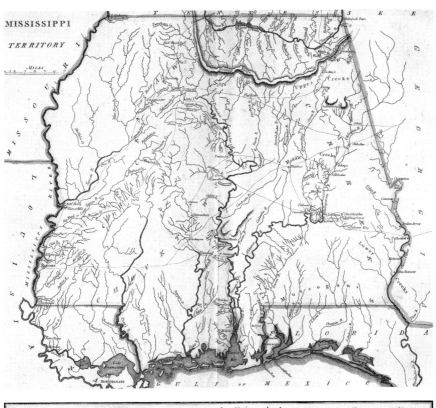

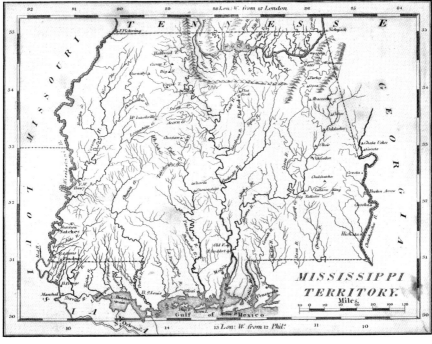

THE MISSISSIPPI TERRITORY

By Fielding Lucas Jr. (1816)
Courtesy of the David Rumsey Map Collection

Appearing in *A New and Elegant General Atlas*, published by Fielding Lucas Jr. and Phillip H. Nicklin, this full-color map was engraved by noted craftsman Henry S. Tanner. It is very similar to the 1814 map published by Matthew Carey in his *General Atlas*, with only minor details in community, road and stream designations to be found. The lag in information on what was happening on the ground in the territory and what cartographers depicted is also evident here, as a number of developing American communities along the Tennessee and Mississippi River Valleys and the Mobile Bay region are not yet depicted.

THE STATE OF MISSISSIPPI AND ALABAMA TERRITORY

By Mathew Carey (1818)
Courtesy of the David Rumsey Map Collection

This is the first map to show the new state of Mississippi and the short-lived Alabama Territory (1817–1819) together. For the first time, some of the counties formed prior to Mississippi's statehood show up on this map, but the listing is incomplete. Madison, Montgomery and Monroe Counties in Alabama, comprising the bulk of the land open for settlement in the eastern section of the territory, had been formed by 1816. The Philadelphia firm of Matthew Carey and Son published the map in the 1818 edition of their *General Atlas*. Francis Shallus did the engraving.

Opposite, top: The Mississippi Territory, by Fielding Lucas Jr., 1816. Courtesy of the David Rumsey Map Collection.

Opposite, bottom: The State of Mississippi and Alabama Territory, by Mathew Carey, 1818. Courtesy of the David Rumsey Map Collection.

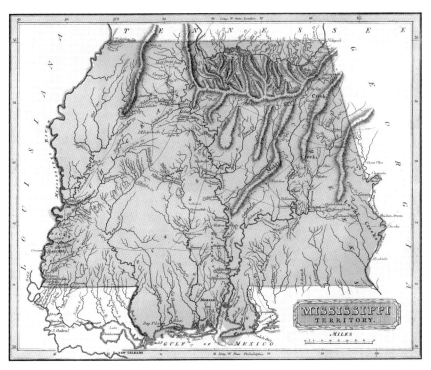

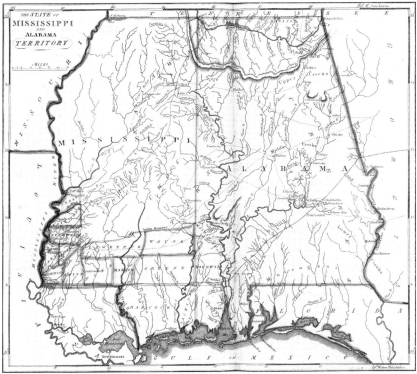

THE STATE OF MISSISSIPPI

By John Melish (1820)
Courtesy of the Library of Congress

Created in 1819 and published in 1820 by Philadelphia mapmaker John Melish, this is believed to be the first map to show Mississippi by itself as an independent state. All of the counties created by the time of statehood are shown, along with several towns that had not previously been depicted on maps of Mississippi. As the map was informed by recently completed surveys, the grid of townships and ranges is overlaid. This map contains a wealth of additional details not previously shown on charts of the region, including the estimated population of the Choctaw and Chickasaw Nations, as well as the path and origins of some of the new roads already crisscrossing the state.

THE STATE OF ALABAMA

By John Melish (1820)
Courtesy of the Library of Congress

Created in 1818 and published in 1820 by John Melish, this is the first known professional map of the new state of Alabama. As with the companion map of Mississippi produced by Melish, the detail is incredible. All county boundaries are shown, as are dozens of American and Native communities previously not represented on maps of the area. A wide variety of roads, forts, ferries and landmarks are listed, such as the site of the Spanish-era Fort Confederation, the land grant given to French refugees along the Tombigbee and Creek towns burned by American forces during the recent Creek War.

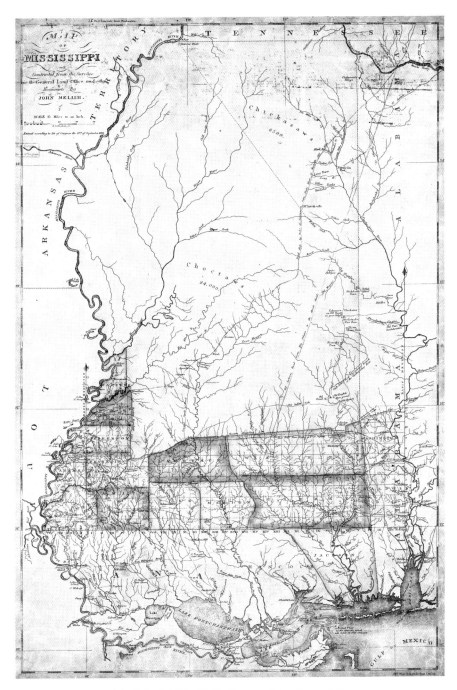

The State of Mississippi, by John Melish, 1820. *Courtesy of the Library of Congress.*

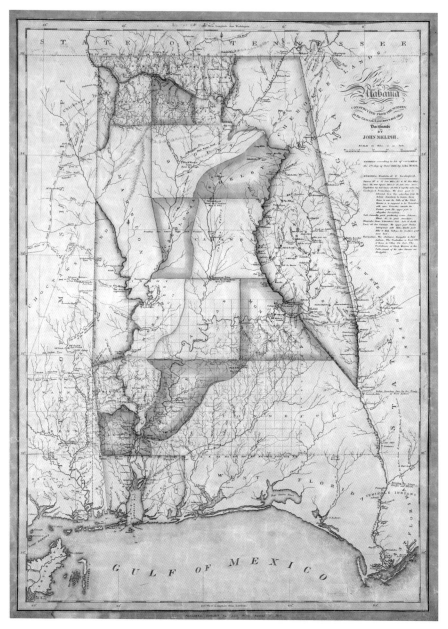

The State of Alabama, by John Melish, 1820. *Courtesy of the Library of Congress.*

MISSISSIPPI

By Henry C. Carey and Isaac Lea (1822)
Courtesy of the David Rumsey Map Collection

The firm of Carey and Lea originally published this map in its *A Complete Historical, Chronological, and Geographical American Atlas* in 1822. Fielding Lucas Jr. did the engraving. The publication is recognized as the first American atlas arranged in the pattern made famous by noted French cartographer and author Emmanuel-Augustin-Dieudonné-Joseph, comte de Las Cases (who published under the pseudonym A. Le Sage). A brief history of the state's colonial and territorial past is found on one side of map, while at the other and along the bottom there is an overview of its form of government, primary cities, rivers and agricultural products; a description of its climate; and a listing of its governors. Enormous swaths of the state still lay under Choctaw and Chickasaw control at the time of this map's creation.

ALABAMA

By Henry C. Carey and Isaac Lea (1822)
Courtesy of the David Rumsey Map Collection

Appearing in the same atlas as the map of Mississippi listed above, this map of Alabama features a variety of pieces of information about the state within the margins. It was engraved by Benjamin Tanner and Fielding Lucas Jr. The map contains rich detail on the young state's communities, roads and waterways. Even some of the key battles in the recent Creek War are indicated. Showing the borders of over thirty counties, the map highlights the fact that relatively little land within the state's borders still lay in Native possession at the time. Within a decade, those few remaining tracts would be carved up into additional counties, and the state would essentially have the configuration we know today.

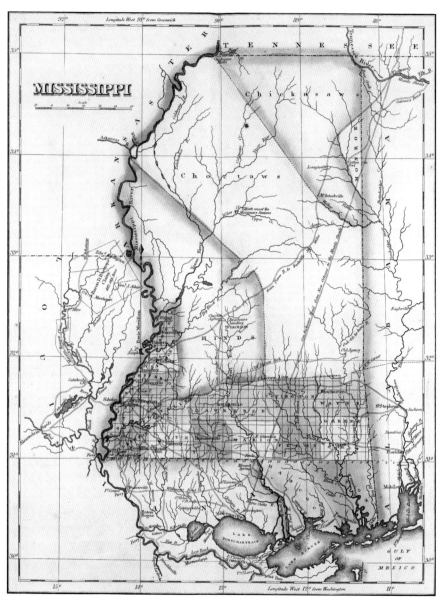

Mississippi, by Henry C. Carey and Isaac Lea, 1822. *Courtesy of the David Rumsey Map Collection.*

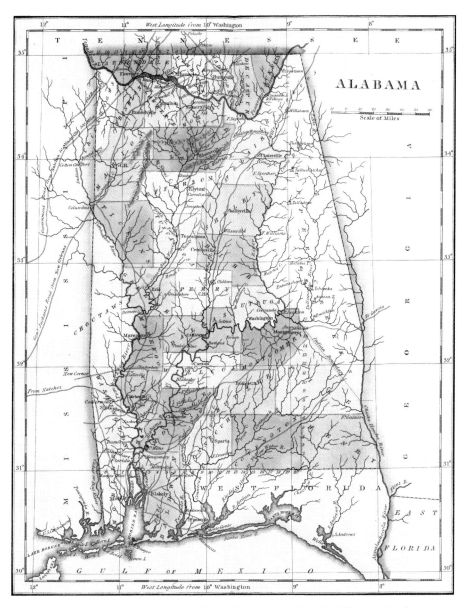

Alabama, by Henry C. Carey and Isaac Lea, 1822. *Courtesy of the David Rumsey Map Collection.*

NOTES

Chapter 1

1. Andrew Ellicott, *The Journal of Andrew Ellicott, Late Commissioner on Behalf of the United States During the Part of the Year 1796, 1797, 1798, 1799 and Part of the Year 1800; for Determining the Boundary Between the United States and the Possessions of His Catholic Majesty in America* (Philadelphia, PA: Budd and Bartam, 1803), 43–44.
2. Robert Haynes, *The Mississippi Territory and the Old Southwest Frontier, 1795–1817* (Lexington: University Press of Kentucky, 2010), 16.
3. Haynes, *Mississippi Territory*, 23–24.
4. Ellicott, *Journal of Andrew Ellicott*, 176; Isaac Guion, "Military Journal of Captain Isaac Gion, 1797–1799," *Annual Report of Mississippi Department of Archives and History*, edited by Dunbar Rowland (Nashville, TN: Bradnon Printing, 1909), 74.
5. Arthur Preston Whitaker, *The Mississippi Question, 1795–1803, A Study on Trade, Politics, and Diplomacy* (New York: D. Appleton Century, 1934), 66–67.
6. Dunbar Rowland, ed., *The Mississippi Territorial Archives, 1798–1803* (Nashville, TN: Press of Brandon), 1:9–10.
7. Haynes, *Mississippi Territory*, 25.
8. Robert Haynes, "The Formation of the Territory," in *A History of Mississippi*, edited by Richard A. McLemore (Jackson: University and College Press of Mississippi, 1973), 179.

Chapter 2

9. Rowland, *Mississippi Territorial Archives*, 25–29.

10. Haynes, "Formation of the Territory," 179.

11. Clarence Carter, ed., *The Territorial Papers of the United States: The Territory of Mississippi, 1798–1817*, vol. 5 (Washington, D.C.: Government Printing Office, 1937), 78–82.

12. Rowland, *Mississippi Territorial Archives*, 185.

13. Rowland, *Mississippi Territorial Archives*, 351–55.

14. Haynes, *Mississippi Territory*, 91.

15. Carter, *Territorial Papers*, 5:654–57.

16. Robert Haynes, "The Road to Statehood," in *A History of Mississippi*, edited by Richard A. McLemore (Jackson: University and College Press of Mississippi, 1973), 217–18.

17. William B. Hamilton, "Politics in the Mississippi Territory," *Huntington Library Quarterly* 11 (1948): 285.

Chapter 3

18. John Spencer Bassett, ed., *Correspondence of Andrew Jackson* (Washington, D.C.: Carnegie Institution of Washington, 1926), 2:82–83.

Chapter 4

19. William B. Hamilton, "Mississippi in 1817: A Sociological and Economic Analysis," *Journal of Mississippi History* 34 (November 1967): 282; Bernard Bailyn, *Voyagers to the West: A Passage in the Peopling of America on the Eve of the Revolution* (New York: Random House, 1986), 480; Charles D. Lowery, "The Great Migration to the Mississippi Territory, 1798–1819," *Journal of Mississippi History* 30 (August 1968): 178.

20. James Graham to Thomas Ruffin, November 9, 1817, in *The Papers of Thomas Ruffin*, vol. 1, edited by J.G. de Roulhac Hamilton (Raleigh, NC: Edwards and Broughton Printing, 1918), 197–99.

21. Lowery, "The Great Migration," 182; Thomas Perkins Abernathy, *The South in the New Nation* (Baton Rouge: Louisiana State Univesity Press, 1961), 466.

22. J.F.H. Claiborne, *Life and Times of General Sam Dale* (New York: Harper and Brothers, 1860), 45, 168.

23. George Rogers, *Memoranda of the Experience, Labor, and Travels of a Universalist Preacher* (Cincinnati, OH: John A. Gurley, 1845), 265.

Chapter 5

24. Ellicott, *Journal of Andrew Ellicott*, 135.

25. Carter, *Territorial Papers*, 5:299.

26. Carter, *Territorial Papers*, 5:322–26.

27. Jeffrey C. Benton, *The Very Worst Road; Traveller's Accounts of Crossing Alabama's Old Creek Indian Territory, 1820–1847* (Eufaula, AL: Historic Chattahoochee Commission, 1998), 70.

Chapter 6

28. Carter, *Territorial Papers*, 5:297–98.

29. Thomas Hart Benton, ed., *Abridgement of the Debates of Congress, from 1789 to 1856*, vol. 4 (New York: D. Appleton and Company, 1857), 411.

30. Carter, *Territorial Papers*, 6:708–17.

BIBLIOGRAPHIC ESSAY

For serious students of Mississippi Territory history, a variety of official records and original documents are readily available as published volumes. By far, the most useful are the edited volumes by Clarence Carter, ed., *The Territorial Papers of the United States: The Territory of Mississippi, 1798–1817* (Washington, D.C.: Government Printing Office, 1937); and Dunbar Rowland, *Mississippi Territorial Archives* (Nashville, TN: Press of Brandon Printing Company, 1905). For documents related to the Alabama Territory, see Clarence Carter, ed., *The Territorial Papers of the United States: The Alabama Territory, 1817–1819* (Washington, D.C.: Government Printing Office, 1952). Many of the most important federal acts as they relate to the territory's development can be found in published volumes as well. These include the edited volumes by Thomas Hart Benton, *Abridgement of the Debates of Congress, from 1789 to 1856*, vol. 4 (New York: D. Appleton and Company, 1857); and *A Century of Lawmaking for a New Nation: U.S. Congressional Documents and Debates, 1774–1875*, Statutes at Large, 14th Congress, 2nd Session, available online through the Library of Congress, at http://memory.loc.gov/ammem/amlaw/lawhome.html. Volumes featuring the text of original documents spanning the entirety of the history of both Mississippi and Alabama also contain material that might be useful to researchers. Among the most comprehensive are Bradley G. Bonds's *Mississippi: A Documentary History* (Jackson: University Press of Mississippi, 2003); and Lucille Griffith's *Alabama: A Documentary History to 1900* (Tuscaloosa: University of Alabama Press, 1972).

There are several books which provide good overviews of the territorial years. Our own book *Old Southwest to Old South: Mississippi, 1798–1840* (Jackson: University Press of Mississippi, 2023) provides a description of several aspects of Mississippi's—and, by extension, Alabama's—territorial experience, as well as its first few decades of statehood. Among the most influential in the compiling of this volume is the monumental volume by Thomas D. Clark and John D.W. Guice, *The Old Southwest, 1795–1830: Frontiers in Conflict* (Norman: University of Oklahoma Press, 1996), a compelling book that remains a standard introductory volume on the larger region of which the Mississippi Territory is a part. Also of use is Reid Badger and Lawrence A. Clayton's edited volume *Alabama and the Borderlands: From Prehistory to Statehood* (Tuscaloosa: University of Alabama Press, 1985); and J. Mills Thornton's *Politics and Power in a Slave Society: Alabama, 1800–1860* (Baton Rouge: Louisiana State University Press, 1978). For the best collection of articles on Alabama's territorial and early statehood periods, see *Alabama from Territory to Statehood* (Montgomery, AL: NewSouth Books, 2019), which contains numerous articles that were published over a period of years in *Alabama Heritage* magazine. For perhaps the most comprehensive reference overview of regional development, see F. Todd Smith's *Louisiana and the Gulf South Frontier 1500–1821* (Baton Rouge: Louisiana State University Press, 2014).

There are too many solid state histories to mention, but among the most informative for this volume were *A History of Mississippi* (Jackson: University and College Press of Mississippi, 1973), edited by Richard A. McLemore; *Mississippi: A History* (Malden, MA: Wiley and Sons, 2015), by Westley F. Busbee Jr.; *Mississippi: An Illustrated History* (Sun Valley, CA: American Historical Press, 2002), by Edward N. Akin and Charles C. Bolton; *Mississippi, A New History* (Jackson: University Press of Mississippi, 2014), by Dennis Mitchell; *Mississippi: A History* (New York: W.W. Norton and Company, 1979), by John Ray Skates; *History of Mississippi: The Heart of the South* (Jackson, MS: S.J. Clarke, 1925), by Dunbar Rowland; *Alabama: The History of a Deep South State* (Tuscaloosa: University of Alabama Press, 1994), by William Warren Rogers, Robert David Ward, Leah Rawls Atkins and Wayne Flynt; *Early Alabama: An Illustrated Guide to the Formative Years, 1798–1826* (Tuscaloosa: University of Alabama Press, 2019), by Mike Bunn; *Clearing the Thickets: A History of Antebellum Alabama* (New Orleans, LA: Quid Pro Quo Books, 2013), by Herbert James Lewis; *Alabama: The Making of an American State* (Tuscaloosa: University of Alabama Press, 2016), by Edwin C. Bridges; *Alabama: A History* (New York: W.W. Norton, 1984), by Virginia Van der Veer Hamilton; *The*

Formative Period in Alabama: 1815–1828 (Tuscaloosa: University of Alabama Press, 1990), by Thomas Perkins Abernathy; and *Rivers of History: Life on the Coosa, Tallapoosa, Cahaba, and Alabama* (Tuscaloosa: University of Alabama Press, 1995), by Harvey H. Jackson III. Two older volumes merit mention as well: J.F.H. Claiborne's *Mississippi as a Province, Territory and State* (Jackson, MS: Power and Barksdale, 1880); and James Albert Pickett's *History of Alabama, and Incidentally of Georgia and Mississippi*, recently published in annotated form by James P. Pate (Montgomery, AL: NewSouth Books, 2018).

Numerous good histories of selected individual regions of the Mississippi Territory have been published. Among the most informative are *The Founding of Alabama: Background and Formative Period in the Great Bend and Madison County* (Tuscaloosa: University of Alabama Press, 2019), by Frances Cabaniss Roberts; Daniel S. Dupre's *Transforming the Cotton Frontier: Madison County, Alabama 1800–1840* (Baton Rouge: Louisiana State University Press, 1997); Charles E. Bryant's *The Tensaw Country North of the Ellicott Line, 1800–1860* (Bay Minette, AL: Lavender Press, 1998); Theodore Bowling Pearson's article "Early Settlement Around Historic McIntosh Bluff: Alabama's First County Seat," *Alabama Review* 23 (October 1970): 243–55; David Byers's article "A History of Early Settlement: Madison County Before Statehood, 1808–1819," *Huntsville Historical Review* (Special Issue, 2008): 42–59; Chriss Doss's article "Early Settlement of Bearmeat Cabin Frontier," *Alabama Review* 22 (October 1969): 270–83; James F. Doster's article "Early Settlements on the Tombigbee and Tensaw Rivers," *Alabama Review* 12 (April 1959): 83–94; T.H. Ball's *A Glance into the Great South-East; Or, Clarke County, Alabama, and Its Surroundings from 1540–1877* (Tuscaloosa, AL: Willo Publishing Co., 1962); John Hawkins Napier III's *Lower Pearl River's Piney Woods: Its Land and People* (University: The University of Mississippi Center for the Study of Southern Culture, 1985); and Charles L. Sullivan's *Mississippi Gulf Coast: Portrait of a People* (Sun Valley, CA: American Historical Press, 1999).

There are also too many histories of individual communities within the areas once part of the Mississippi Territory to mention; they contain information on life within these areas during the territorial era. There are many good books on the important city of Natchez in particular: D. Clayton James's *Antebellum Natchez* (Baton Rouge: Louisiana State University Press, 1993); Noel Polk's *Natchez Before 1830* (Jackson: University Press of Mississippi, 1989); and *Natchez, An Illustrated History* (Natchez, MS: Plantation Publishing, 1992), by David G. Sansing, Sim C. Callon and Carolyn Vance Smith. For information on the legendary and rowdy riverside area below the bluff on which Natchez proper sits, see Edith W. Moore's *Natchez Under-the-*

Hill (Natchez, MS: Southern Historical Publications, 1958); and Virginia Parks Matthias's article "Natchez-Under-the-Hill: As It Developed Under the Influence of the Mississippi River and the Natchez Trace," *Journal of Mississippi History* 7 (1945): 201–21; D. Clayton James's article "Municipal Government in Territorial Natchez," *Journal of Mississippi History* 27 (May 1965). For information on Mobile, see Michael V.R. Thomason, ed., *Mobile: The New History of Alabama's First City* (Tuscaloosa: University of Alabama Press, 2001); Melton McLaurin and Michael Thomason, *Mobile: The Life and Times of a Great Southern City* (Woodland Hills, CA: Windsor Publications, 1981); and Harriet E. Amos, *Cotton City: Urban Development in Antebellum Mobile* (Tuscaloosa: University of Alabama Press, 2001). Though it is well over a century old, Peter J. Hamilton's landmark study *Colonial Mobile: A Historical Study* (New York: Houghton, Mifflin and Company, 1897) is informative and still readily available.

Among the other notable studies of communities with substantial information on the territorial period are: Edward Chambers Betts, *Early History of Huntsville, Alabama 1804–1870* (Montgomery, AL: The Brown Printing Company, 1916); Jay Higginbotham, *Pascagoula: Singing River City* (Mobile, AL: Gill Press, 1967); Jack D. Elliott Jr. and Mary Ann Wells, *Cotton Gin Port: A Frontier Settlement on the Upper Tombigbee* (Jackson, MS: Quail Ridge Press, 2003); Guy B. Braden, "A Jeffersonian Village: Washington, Mississippi," *Journal of Mississippi History* 30 (1968): 135–42; H.G. Hawkins, "History of Port Gibson, Mississippi," *Publications of the Mississippi Historical Society* 10 (1909): 279–99; and C.W. Grafton, "A Sketch of the Old Scotch Settlement at Union Church," *Publications of the Mississippi Historical Society* 9 (1906): 263–71. For detailed accounts of the history of the Vine and Olive Company settlement near what later became Demopolis, Alabama, see Rafe Blaufarb, *Bonapartists in the Borderlands: French Exiles and Refugees on the Gulf Coast, 1815–1835* (Tuscaloosa: University of Alabama Press, 2005); and Eric Saugera, *Reborn in America: French Exiles and Refugees in the United States and the Vine and Olive Adventure, 1815–1865* (Tuscaloosa: University of Alabama Press, 2011). There are a few county-level studies that were helpful in research for this book and deserve mention: Jesse M. Wilkins's article "Early Times in Wayne County," *Publications of the Mississippi Historical Society* 6 (1902): 265–72; and Robert V. Haynes's article "Early Washington County, Alabama," *Alabama Review* 18 (July 1965): 183–200.

Several studies of the migration to the Mississippi Territory were helpful in the writing of this book. Among the best are "The Great Migration to the Mississippi Territory, 1798–1819," *Journal of Mississippi History* 30 (August

1968): 173–92, by Charles D. Lowery; "The Land Rush to Statehood: Alabama Fever," *Alabama Heritage* (Spring 2011): 35–43, by Donna Cox Baker; and "The Pattern of Migration and Settlement on the Southern Frontier," *Journal of Southern History* 11 (May 1945): 147–76, by Frank L. Owsley. For information on land distribution in the territory, see Robert V. Haynes, "The Disposal of Lands in the Mississippi Territory," *Journal of Mississippi History* 24 (October 1962): 226–52; James F. Doster, "Land Titles and Public Land Sales in Early Alabama," *Alabama Review* 16 (April 1963): 108–24; Frances C. Roberts, "Politics and Public Land Disposal in Alabama's Formative Period," *Alabama Review* 22 (July 1969): 163–74; and Alan V. Briceland, "Land, Law, and Politics on the Tombigbee Frontier, 1804," *Alabama Review* 33 (April 1980): 92–124. For intriguing overviews of America's westward expansion in the era, see Bernard Bailyn, *Voyagers to the West: A Passage in the Peopling of America on the Eve of the Revolution* (New York: Random House, 1986); and Ray Allen Billington, *Westward Expansion, A History of the American Frontier* (New York: The Macmillan Company, 1967).

For a unique glimpse at how frontier homes were equipped and what types of property early settlers obtained in carving out a new life for themselves in the Mississippi Territory, see Richard S Lackey, ed., *Frontier Claims in the Lower South* (Baton Rouge, LA: Provincial Press, 1977). Incidentally, concise overviews of French, Spanish and English claims to the Mississippi Territory and their impact in its settlement are provided in several state histories. The complicated affair that arose from Georgia's claims to what became the Mississippi Territory is likewise chronicled in numerous histories of Georgia. For a unique assemblage of primary materials related to these claims, see Edmund C. Burnett, ed., "Papers Related to Bourbon County, Georgia, 1785–1786," *American Historical Review* 15 (October 1909–July 1910): 66–353.

There are numerous studies of travel within the Mississippi Territory. No territorial period path has been more studied than the legendary Natchez Trace. The best of the dozens of accounts of life along its route by far is William C. Davis's *A Way Through the Wilderness: The Natchez Trace and the Civilization of the Southern Frontier* (New York: HarperCollins, 1995). Other notable book-length studies include: Robert M. Coates, *The Outlaw Years: The History of the Land Pirates of the Natchez Trace* (New York: Macauley, 1930); James A. Crutchfield, *The Natchez Trace: A Pictorial History* (Nashville, TN: Rutledge Hill Press, 1985); Jonathan Daniels, *The Devil's Backbone* (New York: McGraw-Hill, 1962); Lena Mitchell Jamison, "The Natchez Trace: A Federal Highway of the Old Southwest," *Journal of Mississippi History* 1 (April 1939): 82–99; George J. Leftwich, "Some Main Traveled Roads,

Including Cross-Sections of Natchez Trace," *Publications of the Mississippi Historical Society* 11 (1916): 463–76; Marius M. Carriere Jr., "Mount Locust Plantation: The Development of Southwest Mississippi During the Frontier Period, 1810–1830," *Journal of Mississippi History* 48 (August 1986): 187–98; Alfred W. Garner, "Folsom's Pigeon Roost, the Nineteenth Century Stage Traveler's Mecca, on the Natchez Trace," *Journal of Mississippi History* 4 (January 1942): 34–37; and two articles by Dawson A. Phelps, "Stands and Travel Accommodations on the Natchez Trace," *Journal of Mississippi History* 11 (January 1949): 1–54, and "Travel On the Natchez Trace," *Journal of Mississippi History* 15 (July 1953): 155–64.

Publications focusing on other noteworthy roads include: Jack D. Elliott Jr., "Three Chopped Way and Representations of Yesteryear," *Journal of Mississippi History* 61 (Fall 1999): 213–36; W.A. Evans, "Gaines Trace in Monroe County, Mississippi," *Journal of Mississippi History* 1 (April 1939): 100–09; Jeffrey C. Benton, *The Very Worst Road; Traveller's Accounts of Crossing Alabama's Old Creek Indian Territory, 1820–1847* (Eufaula, AL: Historic Chattahoochee Commission, 1998); and Henry deLeon Southerland and Jerry E. Brown, *The Federal Road Through Georgia, and the Creek Nation, and Alabama, 1806–1836* (Tuscaloosa: University of Alabama Press, 1990).

Some of the most insightful accounts of life during the territorial and early statehood periods come from the observations of travelers or residents who left memoirs of their experiences traversing the land. Some of the most useful and entertaining are: Reuben Gold Thwaites, *Early Western Travels, 1748–1846* (Cleveland, OH: The Arthur H. Clark Company, 1905); Edouard de Montule, *Montule's Voyage to North America and the West Indies in 1817* (London: Sir Richard Phillips and Company, 1821); Susan Dabney Smedes, *Memorials of a Southern Planter* (Baltimore, MD: Cushing and Bailey, 1888); William Richardson, *Journey from Boston to the Western Country and Mississippi Rivers to New Orleans, 1815–1816* (New York: Valve Pilot Corporation, 1940); Christian Schultz, *Travels on an Inland Voyage Through the States of New York, Pennsylvania, Virginia, Ohio, and Tennessee* (New York: Isaac Riley, 1810); Henry Ker, *Travels Through the Western Interior of the United States* (Elizabethtown, NJ: Ker, 1816); Andrew Oehler, *The Life, Adventures, and Unparalleled Sufferings of Andre Oehler, Containing an Account of His Travels* (Trenton, NJ: D. Fenton, 1811); Orrin Scofield, *Preambulations of Cosmopolite, Or the Travels and Labors of Lorenzo Dow* (Rochester, NY: Scofield, 1842); Jacob Young, *Autobiography of a Pioneer* (Cincinnati, OH: L. Swormstedt and A. Poe, 1857); Abiezer Clark Ramsey, *Memoirs of a Circuit Rider, Being Excerpts from the Life and Times of A.C. Ramsey and Others* (Birmingham, AL: Birmingham-Southern College, 1951);

Francis Baily, *Journal of a Tour in Unsettled Parts of North America in 1796 and 1797* (London: Baily Brothers, 1856); Fortescue Cuming, *Cuming's Sketches of a Tour of the Western Country, 1807–1809* (Pittsburgh, PA: Cramer, Spear, and Richbaum, 1810); Jerry Bryan Lincecum and Edward Hake Phillips, *Adventures of a Frontier Naturalist: The Life and Times of Dr. Gideon Lincecum* (College Station: Texas A&M University Press, 1994); Anne Newport Royall, *Letters from Alabama, on Various Subjects* (Washington, D.C.: Anne Royall, 1830); Clark Hunter, ed., *The Life and Letters of Alexander Wilson* (Philadelphia, PA: American Philosophical Society, 1983); Donald C. Peattie, ed., *Audubon's America: The Narrative and Experiences of John James Audubon* (Boston, MA: Houghton Mifflin, 1940); James Pearse, *A Narrative of the Life of James Pearse* (Rutland, VT: William Fay, 1825); William H. Sparks, *The Memories of Fifty Years* (Macon, GA: J.W. Burke and Company, 1872); Mary J. Welsh, "Recollections of Pioneer Life in Mississippi," *Publications of the Mississippi Historical Society* 4 (1901): 343–56; Gideon Lincecum, "Autobiography of Gideon Lincecum," *Publications of the Mississippi Historical Society* 8 (1905): 443–519; Margaret Ervin Austill, "Life of Margaret Ervin Austill," *Alabama Historical Quarterly* 6 (Spring 1944): 92–98; Richard Breckinridge, "Diary of Richard Breckinridge, 1816," in *Transactions of the Alabama Historical Society, 1898–1899*, edited by Thomas McAdory Owen (Tuscaloosa: Alabama Historical Society, 1904), 142–53; William Darby, *The Emigrant's Guide to the Western and Southwestern States and Territories: Comprising a Geographical and Statistical Description of the States of Louisiana, Mississippi, Tennesseee, Kentucky, and Ohio* (New York: Kirk and Mercein, 1818). For an overview of travel during the period, see Seymour Dunbar, *A History of Travel in America* (New York: Tudor Publishing Company, 1937).

There are numerous full-length biographies or biographical sketches of key players in Mississippi's and Alabama's territorial experience. Among those consulted for this book include: Herbert James Lewis, *Alabama Founders: Fourteen Political and Military Leaders Who Shaped the State* (Tuscaloosa: University of Alabama Press, 2018); Clayton Rand, *Men of Spine in Mississippi* (Gulfport, MS: Dixie Press, 1940); Mack Swearingen, *The Early Life of George Poindexter: A Story of the Old Southwest* (New Orleans, LA: Tulane University Press, 1934); J.F.H. Claiborne, *Life and Times of General Sam Dale* (New York: Harper and Brothers, 1860); Charles S. Sydnor, *A Gentleman of the Old Natchez Region: Benjamin L.C. Wailes* (Durham, NC: Duke University Press, 1938); Robert E. May, *John A. Quitman: Old South Crusader* (Baton Rouge: Louisiana State University Press, 1985); James Paul Pate, ed., *The Reminiscences of George Strother Gaines, Pioneer and Statesman of Early Alabama and Mississippi, 1805–1843*

(Tuscaloosa: University of Alabama Press, 1998); William B. Hamilton, *Anglo-American Law on the Frontier: Thomas Rodney and His Territorial Cases* (Durham, NC: Duke University Press, 1953); Darrel E. Bigham, "From the Green Mountains to the Tombigbee: Henry Hitchcock in Territorial Alabama, 1817–1819," *Alabama Review* 26 (July 1973): 209–28; Alan V. Briceland, "Ephraim Kirby: Mr. Jefferson's Emissary on the Tombigbee-Mobile Frontier in 1804," *Alabama Review* 24 (April 1971): 83–113. There are several biographical studies of noted pioneer scientist William Dunbar, Arthur H. DeRosier Jr.'s *William Dunbar, Scientific Pioneer of the Old Southwest* (Lexington: University Press of Kentucky, 2007) being the latest and most comprehensive. For more on Dunbar's life and times, see Dunbar Rowland, *Life, Letters and Papers of William Dunbar of Elgin, Morayshire, Scotland, and Natchez, Mississippi: Pioneer Scientist of the Southern United States* (Jackson: Press of the Mississippi Historical Society, 1930); Franklin L. Riley, "Sir William Dunbar: The Pioneer of Scientist of Mississippi," *Publications of the Mississippi Historical Society* 2 (1899): 85–111; James R. Dungan, "'Sir' William Dunbar of Natchez Planter, Explorer and Scientist 1792–1810," *Journal of Mississippi History* 24 (October 1961): 211–28. For summary sketches of individual politicians and officials, see Dunbar Rowland, *Courts, Judge, and Lawyers of Mississippi, 1798–1935* (Jackson, MS: Hederman Brothers, 1935); Jo Tice Bloom, "Mississippi's Territorial Delegates," *Journal of Mississippi History* 37 (November 1975): 327–57; Samuel L. Webb and Margaret E. Armbrester, eds., *Alabama Governors: A Political History of the State* (Tuscaloosa: University of Alabama Press, 2001). The online encyclopedias of Alabama (*Encyclopedia of Alabama*, http://www.encyclopediaofalabama.org/) and Mississippi (*Mississippi Encyclopedia*, https://mississippiencyclopedia.org/) contain numeral excellent biographical essays on key individuals from the period as well.

Information on society and culture in the Mississippi Territory can be found in a wide variety of sources. Among the topical overviews consulted in the writing of this volume were: Everett Dick, *The Dixie Frontier: A Social History* (New York: Knopf, 1948); Frank L. Owsley, *Plain Folk of the Old South* (Baton Rouge: Louisiana State University Press, 1949); Walter B. Posey, "The Public Manners of Ante-Bellum Southerners," *Journal of Mississippi History* 19 (October 1957): 219–33; and two outstanding articles by William B. Hamilton, "Mississippi in 1817: A Sociological and Economic Analysis," *Journal of Mississippi History* 34 (November 1967): 270–92, and "The Southwestern Frontier, 1795–1817: An Essay in Social History," *Journal of Southern History* 10 (1944): 389–403. Christopher Morris's *Becoming Southern:*

The Evolution of a Way of Life, Warren County and Vicksburg, Mississippi, 1770–1860 (New York: Oxford University Press, 1995) offers a unique local study of culture and society. Studies focusing specifically on family life and women include: Joan E. Cashin, *A Family Venture: Men and Women on the Southern Frontier* (New York: Oxford University Press, 1991); and Donna Elizabeth Sedevie, "The Prospect of Happiness: Women, Divorce and Property," *Journal of Mississippi History* 52 (February 1995): 189–206. There are several studies specifically investigating life on the Mississippi River, none more useful in understanding the rivermen of legend than Michael Allen's *Western Rivermen, 1763–1861: Ohio and Mississippian Boatmen Myth of the Alligator Horse* (Baton Rouge: Louisiana State University Press, 1990); and Walter Blair and Franklin J. Meine's *Half Horse, Half Alligator: The Growth of the Mike Fink Legend* (Chicago, IL: University of Chicago Press, 1956). For an excellent overview of the history of the development of the steamboat and its impact, see Adam I. Kane, *The Western River Steamboat* (College Station: Texas A&M University Press, 2004). Also of use is S.L. Kotar and J.E. Gessler, *The Steamboat Era: A History of Fulton's Folly on American Rivers, 1807–1860* (Jefferson, NC: McFarland and Company, 2009). For a look at steamboats on the Tombigbee, see Rufus Ward, *The Tombigbee River Steamboats: Rollodores, Dead Heads, and Side-Wheelers* (Charleston, SC: The History Press, 2010). Dueling as evidence of a unique priority given to the concept of honor is discussed in Wilmuth S. Rutledge, "Dueling in Antebellum Mississippi," *Journal of Mississippi History* 26 (1964): 181–91. Bertram Wyatt-Brown's landmark study, *Southern Honor: Ethics and Behavior in the Old South* (London: Oxford University Press, 2007), remains the single best source of information on this aspect of antebellum society. For a unique study of food supply during the period, see Sam Bowers Hilliard, *Hog Meat and Hoecake: A Geographical View of Food Supply in the Heart of the Old South* (Madison: University of Wisconsin–Madison, 1966).

Agriculture was fundamental to virtually every aspect of the daily life of most residents of the Mississippi Territory, and information relating to its practice can be found in most general histories of the region. Among the studies focusing specifically on agriculture during the time period consulted for this book were: John Hebron Moore, *The Emergence of the Cotton Kingdom in the Old Southwest* (Baton Rouge: Louisiana State University Press, 1998); James L. Watkins, *King Cotton: A Historical and Statistical Review, 1790–1808* (New York: James J. Watkins and Sons, 1908); Charles S. Davis, *Cotton Kingdom in Alabama* (Philadelphia, PA: Porcupine Press, 1974); John D.W. Guice, "Cattle Raisers of the Old Southwest: A Reinterpretation," *Western Historical Quarterly* 8 (April 1977): 166–77; and Forrest McDonald and Grady McWhiney, "The

Antebellum Southern Herdsman: A Reinterpretation," *Journal of Southern History* 41 (May 1975): 147–66. There are few studies of the banking system in the territorial years, which was integrally connected to land use and sale. William H. Brantley's *Banking in Alabama, 1816–1860* (Birmingham, AL: Oxmoor Press, 1961) provides some overview information on the beginnings of banking in the territorial period. For detailed information on one of the most influential early banks, see Marvin Bentley, "The State Bank of Mississippi: Monopoly Bank on the Frontier (1809–1830)," *Journal of Mississippi History* 40 (November 1978): 297–318.

For studies of entertainment on the frontier, see Herbert Asbury, *Sucker's Progress; An Informal History of Gambling in America* (New York: Thunder's Mouth Press, 1938); Joseph Miller Free, "The Ante-Bellum Theater of the Old Natchez Region," *Journal of Mississippi History* 5 (April 1941): 14–27; and Laura D.S. Harrell's articles on horse racing, "Horse Racing in the Old Natchez District," *Journal of Mississippi History* 13 (1951): 123–37, and "Jockey Clubs and Race Tracks in Antebellum Mississippi," *Journal of Mississippi History*, 28 (November 1966): 304–18.

A concise overview of medical practice during the time can be found in Lucie Robertson Bridgforth's "Medicine in Antebellum Mississippi," *Journal of Mississippi History* 46 (May 1984): 82–107. For a good overview of the disease of yellow fever and its spread, methods of control and influence in southern history, see Margaret Humphreys, *Yellow Fever and the South* (Baltimore, MD: Johns Hopkins University Press, 1999).

Numerous studies of the institution of slavery in the South were consulted for this book, most of the authors of which view the practice from a regional lens and focus on the later antebellum period. Among the most thorough of these examinations as it regards the daily life of enslaved people are the landmark volumes by John W. Blassingame, *The Slave Community: Plantation Life in the Antebellum South* (New York: Oxford University Press, 1979); Eugene D. Genovese, *Roll Jordan Roll: The World the Slaves Made* (New York: Random House, 1976); Kenneth M. Stampp, *Peculiar Institution: Slavery in the Ante-Bellum South* (New York: Random House, 1989); and Elizabeth Fox-Genovese, *Within the Plantation Household: Black and White Women of the Old South* (Chapel Hill: University of North Carolina Press, 1988). Statewide studies consulted include: Charles S. Sydnor, *Slavery in Mississippi* (Baton Rouge: Louisiana State University Press, 1966); David J. Libby, *Slavery and Frontier Mississippi, 1720–1835* (Jackson: University Press of Mississippi, 2004); and James Benson Sellers, *Slavery in Alabama* (Tuscaloosa: University of Alabama Press, 1950). Several narratives of individual enslaved people who lived during the era exist and helped frame our overview of life within the institution as well. Those consulted for this book include Andrew Waters, ed., *Prayin to Be Set Free: Personal Accounts of Slavery in Mississippi* (Winston-Salem, NC: John F. Blair, 2002); and William J. Anderson, *Life and Narrative of William J. Anderson: Twenty Four Years a Slave* (Chicago, IL: Daily Tribune Book and Job Printing Office, 1857). For information on the slave patrol system in early Mississippi, see J. Michael Crane, "Controlling the Night: Perceptions of the Slave Patrol System in Mississippi," *Journal of Mississippi History* 61 (Summer 1999): 119–36. For a brief history of the notorious Forks of the Road slave market, see Jim Barnett and Clark Burkett, "The Forks of the Road Slave Market at Natchez," *Journal of Mississippi History* 63 (Fall 2001): 169–88.

For information on education in the Mississippi Territory, see Edward Mayes, *History of Education in Mississippi* (Washington, D.C.: Government Printing Office, 1999); Michael V. O'Shea, *Public Education in Mississippi* (Jackson, MS: Jackson Printing Company, 1927); Richard A. McLemore, "The Roots of Higher Education in Mississippi," *Journal of Mississippi History* 26 (1964): 207–18; Alfred Benjamin Butts, "Public Education," *Publications of the Mississippi Historical Society, Centenary Series* 3 (1919): 2–66; Margaret DesChamps Moore, ed., "Early Schools and Churches in Natchez," *Journal of Mississippi History* 24 (October 1962): 253–55; and Julia Huston Nguyen, "The Value of Learning: Education and Class in Antebellum Natchez," *Journal of Mississippi History* 61 (Fall 1999): 303–19.

There are several studies of Jefferson College, the lone institution of higher learning that operated in the territory: W.T. Blain, *Education in the Old Southwest: A History of Jefferson College, Washington, Mississippi* (Washington, MS: Friends of Jefferson College, 1976); J.K. Morrison, "Early History of Jefferson College," *Publications of the Mississippi Historical Society* 2 (1899): 183; Noel Polk, *Natchez Before 1830* (Jackson: University Press of Mississippi, 1989); J.K. Morrison, "Early History of Jefferson College," *Publications of the Mississippi Historical Society* 2 (1899): 179–88; and William B. Hamilton, "Jefferson College and Education in Mississippi, 1798–1817," *Journal of Mississippi History* 3 (1941): 259–76.

Religion in the Mississippi Territory is a relatively well-studied subject. By far, the best single comprehensive source on the subject is Randy J. Sparks's *Religion in Mississippi* (Jackson: University Press of Mississippi, 2001). Other useful overviews include: John G. Jones, *Concise History of the Introduction of Protestantism into Mississippi and the Southwest* (St. Louis, MO: Pinckard, 1866); Walter Brownlow Posey, *Frontier Mission: A History of Religion West of the Southern Appalachians to 1861* (Lexington: University of Kentucky Press, 1966);

Margaret Deschamps Moore, "Protestantism in the Mississippi Territory," *Journal of Mississippi History* 29 (November 1967): 358–70; and Frances Allen Cabaniss and James A. Cabaniss, "Religion in Ante-Bellum Mississippi," *Journal of Mississippi History* 6 (October 1944): 191–224. For information on individual Christian churches, see Jesse L. Boyd, *A Popular History of the Baptists in Mississippi* (Jackson, MS: Baptist Press, 1930); Z.T. Leavell and T.J. Bailey, *A Complete History of Mississippi Baptists from the Earliest Times* (Jackson: Mississippi Baptist Publishing Company, 1903); Z.T. Leavell, "Early Beginnings of Baptists in Mississippi," *Publications of the Mississippi Historical Society* 4 (1901): 245–53; Walter B. Posey, "The Early Baptist Church in the Lower Southwest," *Journal of Southern History* 10 (May 1944): 161–73; Nash K. Burger and Charlotte Capers, "Episcopal Clergy of Mississippi, 1790–1940," *Journal of Mississippi History* 8 (April, 1946): 59–66; Walter B. Posey, "Advance of Methodism into the Lower Southwest," *Journal of Southern History* 2 (November 1936): 439–52; Ray Holder, *William Winans: Methodist Leader in Antebellum Mississippi* (Jackson: University Press of Mississippi, 1977); Walter B. Posey, *The Presbyterian Church in the Old Southwest, 1778–1838* (Richmond, VA: John Knox Press, 1952); T.L. Haman, "Beginnings of Presbyterianism in Mississippi," *Publications of the Mississippi Historical Society* 10 (1909): 203–21; Walter B. Posey, "The First Session Book of the Oldest Presbyterian Church in Mississippi," *Journal of Mississippi History* 10 (April 1948): 132–49; James William Marshall and Robert Strong, *The Presbyterian Church in Alabama: A Record of the Growth of the Presbyterian Church from its Beginnings in 1811 in the Eastern Portion of the Mississippi Territory to the Centennial of the Synod of Alabama in 1936* (Montgomery: Presbyterian Historical Society of Alabama, 1977); Richard O. Gerow, *Catholicity in Mississippi* (Natchez, MS: N.P., 1939). For information on the Mississippi Territory's very small Jewish population, see Rabbi Leo Turitz and Evelyn Turitz, *Jews in Early Mississippi* (Jackson: University Press of Mississippi, 1995).

The complicated story behind the establishment of the Mississippi-Alabama boundary is detailed in several articles. The best is Franklin L. Riley's "Location of the Boundaries of Mississippi," *Publications of the Mississippi Historical Society* 3 (1900): 167–84. See also, Richard A. McLemore, "The Division of the Mississippi Territory," *Journal of Mississippi History* 5 (1943): 79–82; Peter J. Hamilton, "Running Mississippi's South Line," *Publications of the Mississippi Historical Society* 2 (1899): 157–68; Richard and Nannie McLemore, "The Birth of Mississippi," *The Journal of Mississippi History* 39 (November 1967): 255–69; J.M. White, "Territorial Growth of Mississippi," *Publications of the Mississippi Historical Society* 2 (1899): 125–34.

There are several good studies of the framing of the first constitutions of Mississippi and Alabama and the beginnings of state government: "The Framing of Mississippi's First Constitution," *Journal of Mississippi History* 29 (November 1967): 301–27, by Wilbourne Magruder Drake; "The Journal of the Constitutional Convention of 1817," *Journal of Mississippi History* 29 (November 1967): 443–504, edited by William F. Winter; "The Birth of Mississippi," *The Journal of Mississippi History* 39 (November 1967): 255–69, edited by Richard McLemore and Nannie McLemore; *Constitutional Development in Alabama, 1798–1901: A Study in Politics, the Negro, and Sectionalism* (Spartanburg, SC: The Reprint Company, 1978), by Malcolm Cook McMillan; "The Alabama Constitution of 1819: A Study of Constitution-Making on the Frontier," *The Alabama Review* 3 (October 1950): 263–85, also by Malcolm Cook McMillan; *Journal of the Convention of the Alabama Territory* (Huntsville, AL: John Boardman, 1819); Leah Atkins, "The First Legislative Session: The General Assembly of Alabama, Huntsville, 1819," *Alabama Review* 23 (January 1970): 30–44; "Establishment of the Alabama Territory," *Alabama Historical Quarterly* 24 (Spring 1962): 97–128; and "More or Less Arbitrary: The Location of the Alabama-Mississippi Border," in *Alabama From Territory to Statehood* (Montgomery, AL: NewSouth Books, 2019), 16–25, by Mike Bunn. See also, Laura D.S. Harrell, "Imprints Toward Statehood," *Journal of Mississippi History* 29 (November 1967): 429–42.

For information on the selection of the early capitals of Alabama and life within them, see William H. Brantley, *Three Capitals: A Book About the First Three Capitals of Alabama* (Tuscaloosa: University of Alabama Press, 1976); Herbert James Lewis, *Lost Capitals of Alabama* (Charleston, SC: The History Press, 2014); and Nan Fairley, "The Lost Capitals of St. Stephens and Cahawba," *Alabama Heritage* (Spring 1998): 18–31.

For an overview of the controversy over the ownership of West Florida and its role in territorial period politics, see William C. Davis. *The Rogue Republic: How Would-Be Patriots Staged the Shortest Revolution in American History* (New York: Houghton Mifflin Harcourt, 2011); Isaac J. Cox, *The West Florida Controversy, 1798–1813* (Baltimore, MD: Johns Hopkins, 1918); and Junius P. Rodriguez, ed., *The Louisiana Purchase: A Historical and Geographical Encyclopedia* (Santa Barbara, CA: ABC-Clio, 2002).

There are too many sources to mention for information on Native cultures in the Mississippi Territory. Some of those consulted for this book include: James Taylor Carson, *Searching for the Bright Path: The Mississippi Choctaws from Prehistory to Removal* (Lincoln: University of Nebraska Press, 1999); Ernest Trice Thompson, *Presbyterian Missions in the Southern United States* (Richmond,

VA: Presbyterian Committee of Publication, 1934); Clara Sue Kidwell, *Choctaws and Missionaries in Mississippi, 1818–1918* (Norman: University of Oklahoma Press, 1995); James F. Barnett Jr., *Mississippi's American Indians* (Jackson: University Press of Mississippi, 2012); Claudio Saunt, *A New Order of Things: Property, Power, and the Transformation of the Creek Indians, 1733–1816* (New York: Cambridge University Press, 1999); Greg O'Brien, *Choctaws in a Revolutionary Age, 1750–1830* (Lincoln: University of Nebraska Press, 2002); Kathryn E. Holland Braund, *Deerskins and Duffels: The Creek Indian Trade With Anglo-America, 1685–1815* (Lincoln: University of Nebraska Press, 1993); Steven C. Hahn, *Invention of the Creek Nation, 1670–1763* (Lincoln: University of Nebraska Press, 2004); Robbie Ethridge, *Creek Country: The Creek Indians and Their World* (Chapel Hill: University of North Carolina Press, 2004).

For information on the watershed Creek War and War of 1812, which transformed the territory's trajectory, see Mike Bunn and Clay Williams, *Battle for the Southern Frontier: The Creek War and the War of 1812* (Charleston, SC: The History Press, 2008); Howard T. Weir, *A Paradise of Blood: The Creek War of 1813–14* (Yardley, PA: Westsholme Publishing, 2016); Peter Cozzens, *A Paradise of Blood: Andrew Jackson, the Creek Indians, and the Epic War for the American South* (New York: Knopf, 2023); Sean Michael O'Brien, *In Bitterness and Tears: Andrew Jackson's Destruction of the Creeks and Seminoles* (Westport, CT: Praeger, 2003); Frank Owsley Jr., *Struggle for the Gulf Borderlands: The Creek War and the Battle of New Orleans 1812–1815* (Tuscaloosa: University of Alabama Press, 1981); Gregory Waselkov, *A Conquering Spirit: Fort Mims and the Redstick War of 1813–1814* (Tuscaloosa: University of Alabama Press, 2006); and Henry S. Halbert and Timothy H. Ball, *The Creek War of 1813 and 1814* (Chicago, IL: Donahue and Henneberry, 1895). For books specifically focusing on the pivotal Battle of New Orleans, see Robert Remini, *The Battle of New Orleans, Andrew Jackson and America's First Military Victory* (New York: Penguin Books, 1999); and William C. Davis, *The Greatest Fury: The Battle of New Orleans and the Rebirth of America* (New York: Dutton Caliber, 2019).

There are numerous excellent biographies about the pivotal national political figure during the territorial years, Andrew Jackson. Among those consulted for this book were Robert Remini, *Andrew Jackson, The Course of American Empire, 1767–1821* (New York: Harper and Row, 1977); H.W. Brands, *Andrew Jackson* (New York: Doubleday, 2005); and Harold D. Moser and Sharon McPheron's edited volumes of Jackson's correspondence, *The Papers of Andrew Jackson* (Knoxville: University of Tennessee Press, 1980).

ABOUT THE AUTHORS

Mike Bunn serves as director of Historic Blakeley State Park in Spanish Fort, Alabama. He is the author and coauthor of several books, including *Fort Stoddert: American Sentinel on the Mobile River, 1799–1814*; *Fourteenth Colony: The Forgotten Story of the Gulf South During America's Revolutionary Era*; *The Assault on Fort Blakeley: "The Thunder and Lightning of Battle"*; and *This Southern Metropolis: Life in Antebellum Mobile*. Mike is chair of the Baldwin County Historic Development Commission, treasurer of the Friends of Old Mobile, a member of the board of the Alabama Historical Association and editor of *Muscogiana*, the journal of the Muscogee County (GA) Genealogical Society.

Clay Williams graduated from Mississippi State University with a bachelor's degree in political science ('93) and a master's degree in history and public policy administration ('95). From 1999 to 2022, he was employed with the Mississippi Department of Archives and History, where he served in a number of positions, such as Old Capitol Museum director and sites administrator. He has cowritten two

books, *Battle for the Southern Frontier, the Creek War and the War of 1812* and *Old Southwest to Old South: Mississippi 1798–1840.* He currently serves as program manager for the Osher Lifelong Learning Institute at the University of Alabama in Huntsville.

Visit us at
www.historypress.com